TURNING THE SOIL

Turning the Soil

250 Years of Vermont Agriculture

Roger Allbee

Published by White River Press
Amherst, Massachusetts

in cooperation with

Center for Research on Vermont
University of Vermont

Published by White River Press
PO Box 3561, Amherst, MA 01004
www.whiteriverpress.com

ISBN: 979-8-88545-023-2

Book and Cover Design by Douglas Lufkin
Lufkin Graphic Designs, Norwich, VT 05055
www.lufkingraphics.com

Library of Congress Cataloging-in-Publication Data

Names: Allbee, Roger, 1945- author.
Title: Turning the soil : 250 years of Vermont agriculture / Roger Allbee.
Other titles: 250 years of Vermont agriculture
Description: Amherst, Massachusetts : White River Press, [2025]
Identifiers: LCCN 2024054305 | ISBN 9798885450232 (paperback)
Subjects: LCSH: Agriculture--Vermont--History.
Classification: LCC S451.V5 A45 2025 | DDC 630.9743--dc23/eng/20250123
LC record available at https://lccn.loc.gov/2024054305

Contents

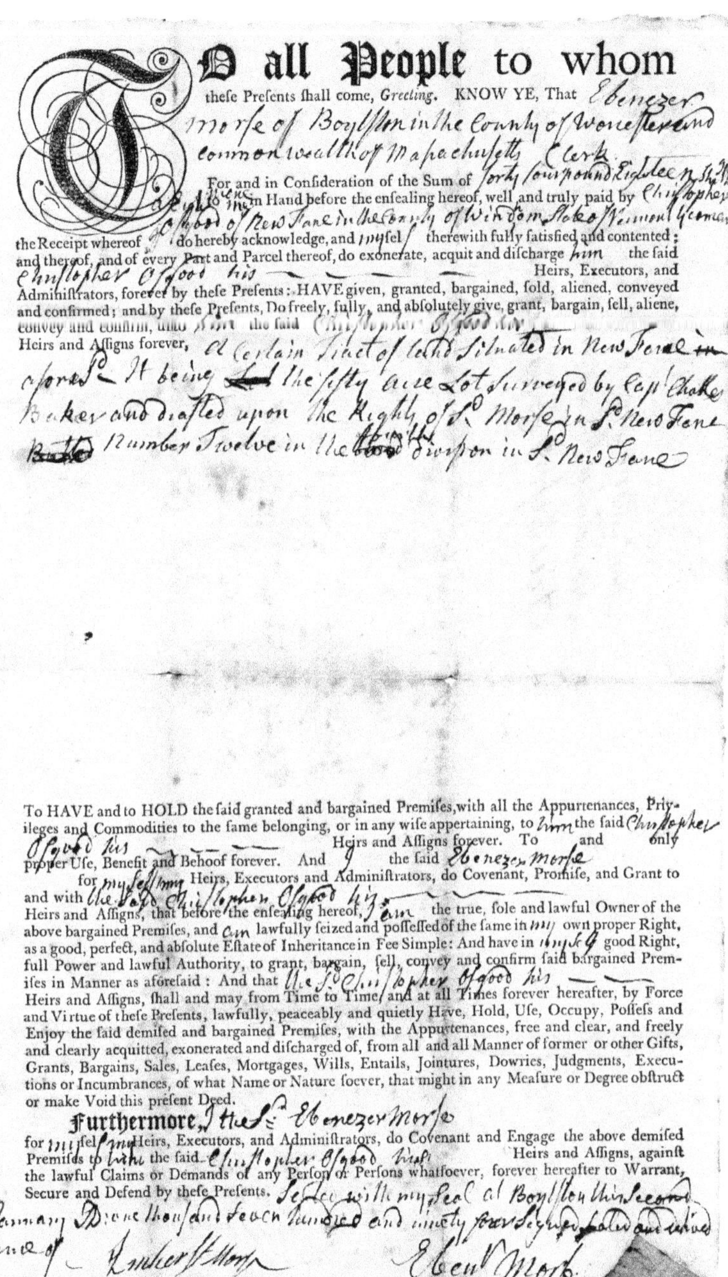

TO all People to whom

these Presents shall come, Greeting. KNOW YE, That *Ebenezer Morse of Boylston in the County of Worcester and commonwealth of Massachusetts Clerk* For and in Consideration of the Sum of *forty four pound Eighteen Sh* in Hand before the ensealing hereof, well and truly paid by *Christopher Osgood of New Fane in the County of Windom State of Vermont Yeoman* the Receipt whereof *I* do hereby acknowledge, and *myself* therewith fully satisfied and contented: and thereof, and of every Part and Parcel thereof, do exonerate, acquit and discharge *him* the said *Christopher Osgood his* Heirs, Executors, and Administrators, forever by these Presents: HAVE given, granted, bargained, sold, aliened, conveyed and confirmed; and by these Presents, Do freely, fully, and absolutely give, grant, bargain, sell, aliene, convey and confirm, unto *him* the said *Christopher Osgood his* Heirs and Assigns forever, *A Certain Tract of land Situated in New Fane in aforesd It being the fifty acre Lot Surveyed by Capt Chase Baker and drafted upon the Right of Dr Morse in Sd New Fane Number Twelve in the third division in Sd New Fane*

To HAVE and to HOLD the said granted and bargained Premises, with all the Appurtenances, Privileges and Commodities to the same belonging, or in any wise appertaining, to *him* the said *Christopher Osgood his* Heirs and Assigns forever. To and only proper Use, Benefit and Behoof forever. And *I* the said *Ebenezer Morse* for *myself my* Heirs, Executors and Administrators, do Covenant, Promise, and Grant to and with *the said Christopher Osgood his* Heirs and Assigns, that before the ensealing hereof, *I am* the true, sole and lawful Owner of the above bargained Premises, and *am* lawfully seized and possessed of the same in *my* own proper Right, as a good, perfect, and absolute Estate of Inheritance in Fee Simple: And have in *myself* good Right, full Power and lawful Authority, to grant, bargain, sell, convey and confirm said bargained Premises in Manner as aforesaid: And that *the Sd Christopher Osgood his* Heirs and Assigns, shall and may from Time to Time, and at all Times forever hereafter, by Force and Virtue of these Presents, lawfully, peaceably and quietly Have, Hold, Use, Occupy, Possess and Enjoy the said demised and bargained Premises, with the Appurtenances, free and clear, and freely and clearly acquitted, exonerated and discharged of, from all and all Manner of former or other Gifts, Grants, Bargains, Sales, Leases, Mortgages, Wills, Entails, Jointures, Dowries, Judgments, Executions or Incumbrances, of what Name or Nature soever, that might in any Measure or Degree obstruct or make Void this present Deed.

Furthermore, *I the Sd Ebenezer Morse* for *myself my* Heirs, Executors, and Administrators, do Covenant and Engage the above demised Premises *to him* the said *Christopher Osgood his* Heirs and Assigns, against the lawful Claims or Demands of any Person or Persons whatsoever, forever hereafter to Warrant, Secure and Defend by these Presents. *Sealed with my Seal at Boylston this Second*

day of January AD one thousand seven hundred and ninety four Signed Sealed and delivered
in presence of

Amherst Morse

Annis Morse

Ebenr Morse

Original deed to Osgood Farm

Preface

MY TWIN BROTHER, RON, AND I were born in a hospital in Brattleboro, Vermont, in 1945, just as World War II ended. At that time, the West River Valley did not have a healthcare facility, so my dad, a farmer, had to drive my mother late on a cold and snowy night to the only hospital in the area to give birth to twins. Along with two older siblings, we grew up in Brookline, a small farming town that was more like a village. When I was born, the population was just over 100, in a valley six miles long by two to three miles wide, totaling 17 square miles. A creek, Grassy Brook, runs through the town in a narrow valley. My childhood was not just a vanishing remnant of the 19th century, but a living connection to the land and the generations who have worked it. Our farm, a sprawling, extended-family compound, was a testament to the deep roots that bind us to Vermont. It was a life built on the foundation of many generations who stayed in Vermont and adapted to changes brought on by national and world events. These ties, reaching back three centuries, are not just historical facts, but a part of me, shaping my life professionally, personally, and culturally.

Vermont has always had a rich agricultural history, with many products harvested from the land. Change has been inevitable, arising from many factors, including transportation, geography, soil types, competition, markets, family values, management skills, public policies and programs, and research and education. This book attempts to review the reasons that change has occurred and how it continues today. In 2011, after my work as Vermont Secretary of Agriculture, I began writing a blog called *What Ceres Says*. The blog focuses on the agricultural history of Vermont beginning in the 1760s, after the French and Indian Wars. My passion for the blog and for this book stems from both my experience in working professionally on agricultural and land-use policies at many levels in and outside of government, as well as the background of my own family.

My ancestors settled in the small town of Newfane in southern Vermont in 1768 and started a farm nearby in Brookline in 1788. The farm still exists, owned by my cousin, and through many generations, it has endured the changes that have taken place in agriculture in the region and the state. The farm has transformed itself over that time to survive. Other farms in the area no longer exist. I grew up on my grandfather's hillside dairy farm nearby, which represented many of the dairy farms in the state and the area at the time. Like many other dairies, my grandfather's dairy farm went out of production when the bulk tank requirement for dairy farmers was instituted during the late 1950s and early 1960s.

Early settlers understood the rigors of working the land; many were subsistence farmers who depended on selling potash and bartering goods from its value. Later came the golden days of grain production in the Champlain Valley, the raising of prized Merino sheep in the early to mid-1800s, followed by dairy with butter and cheese production and the essentially fluid milk to supply the Boston market. During these changes, farmers across the state engaged in diverse seasonal enterprises that would have included maple, apples, and potatoes; horses, poultry, and eggs; hemp, hops, and even spirits. Vermont farmers have never been immune from regional, national, or international influences. While many adapted to market demands, reinventing themselves to survive, many more did not. Early farms were relatively self-sufficient in meeting their food needs before becoming more specialized. Over time, increased efficiencies in transportation and continued consolidation in the food system have increased the economic challenges Vermont farmers face today.

My hope is that this book will provide readers with a deeper understanding of the challenges and opportunities facing Vermont's farmers. I will guide the reader through critical periods in Vermont's agricultural history, sharing stories of people and the events of their time.

We will delve into the reasons behind changes in farming practices and prospects, and what this history can teach us about the future of farm and land use in our state. While some may argue that Vermont is no longer an agricultural state, the majority of the population still values open space and the working landscape. The question then becomes, how will future changes affect farming and the working landscape in Vermont? How will climate change and changes in consumer behavior impact the environment for agriculture?

I am deeply passionate about Vermont, our farming communities, and the past, present, and future of our working landscape. I am continually inspired by the resilience of our hardworking farmers and their families, who, despite myriad challenges and changes, find ways to survive. Whether they operate organic or non-organic farms, part-time or full-time, their dedication and perseverance are truly commendable.

CHAPTER ONE

Clearing the Land, Subsistence Farming, and the Potash Trade

IN THE SPRING OF 1766 my family's records show that my ancestor Jonathan Park set off north from Worcester County, Massachusetts, "with tinder box and kettle slung over his shoulder, to seek his fortune in 'Hampshire Grants.'" New Hampshire's then governor Wentworth, eager to expand into territory west of the Connecticut River, was offering cheap "land grants" to all comers. Park, pursuing this opportunity, halted in the frontier town of Fane—now Newfane, Vermont—selecting lots on a hilltop in the center of the land. Park first cleared what is known as Old Newfane Hill Common, and then, in the summer of 1768, began a clearing at Fayetteville (now Newfane Village). He proceeded to build what would become the first frame house in town, covering the hand-hewn frame with hemlock bark.[1]

Park wasn't alone. After England won possession of Canada with the Treaty of Paris in 1763, settlers from southern New England began moving north in search of plentiful, fertile land, which was lacking in Massachusetts and Connecticut.

Vermont's early settlers were hardy, accustomed from childhood to the use of axes and guns; they were full of an ambitious purpose to found homes and communities of their own. Between 1780 and 1800, the settler population of Vermont grew from 30,000 to 150,000.[2] The vast majority were of British origin: of the roughly 85,000 Vermonters reported in the

1790 census, some 81,200 of them were English and another 2,600 were reported to be Scots.

Bird's eye view of Newfane, Vermont

For thousands of years before European settlement, the Abenaki people had lived on the land and the waters. They grew crops in association with settled villages on the Missisquoi, Winooski, and Connecticut Rivers. These earliest habitants of the land practiced an itinerant form of agriculture, seasonally rotating among various agricultural clearings.[3] For example, below the soil of the Intervale in Burlington, where the Winooski River becomes a delta, is a 5,000 year record of Abenaki history. It shows that the land was used seasonally for hunting, fishing, gathering, and growing food. It is likely the Abenaki grew the three sisters—corn, beans, and squash—as well as tobacco and sweetgrass, their sacred crops.[4]

From the perspective of the European settlers, the northern New England forests were empty and ripe for the taking. After clearing the land, the settlers grew a variety of crops between the stumps. Corn was a staple crop, along with beans, pumpkins, turnips and parsnips, a few kinds of potatoes, and wheat, barley, and buckwheat. Often a farmstead would boast at least a cow and a pig, too. Sheep were kept for wool. Flax was raised and cultivated for its fiber and made into clothes.

Ira Allen, one of the state's founders, hailed Vermont's lush land and resources in 1796. While in England, he wrote a letter to the Duke of Portland on that subject:

> The soil with a little cultivation supplies inhabitants with all the necessaries of life in abundance, such as wheat, oats, rye, beans, barley. They have no necessity to introduce foreign grasses, where every hill and valley affords an abundance of herbage spontaneously, and every plain, permitted to remain a few months untouched, becomes a meadow. The woods also produce other fruits in plenty, some of which you must pamper in your hothouses in England. Our climate is mild, our soil fertile, our inhabitants industrious, our provisions abundant and cheap, and we are determined to avail ourselves of these blessings and to hand them down at least unimpaired to our children.[5]

The Rev. Samuel Williams, writing at about the same time, proclaimed of the agricultural conditions, "In no part of the United States does the farmer meet with more success in raising sheep" than in Vermont. The climate was ideal, the reverend wrote, and the rich pastures on which they grazed gave an extra "sweetness to the meat and richness to the fleece."[6]

"In no place does flax succeed better than on the new lands," he added. "The manufacture of maple sugar is also an article of great importance." Grains, sheep, and maple, as well as dairy, would all feature prominently in Vermont's agricultural history, but the state's first major export was a product few today have heard of: potash.

Potash: Vermont's First Economy

Potash—and later pearlash—were valuable items to the export trade with England. The British needed potash and pearlash for glass making and other manufacturing processes, as well as for soap to wash the wool of their sheep. At the time settlers began clearing land in Vermont, Britain had depleted its own timber resources and sources in other regions of the world were being challenged. To stimulate the production of this early industrial chemical, the English Parliament passed an act urging New World settlers to manufacture these salts in 1751. England went so far as to send experts and manuals on potash making to the colonies. By 1756 the crown had waived all duty taxes on the products from America.

Potash is a chemical salt made by burning hardwood trees to ashes, soaking the ashes in water, and boiling the resulting lye solution down to a powder. Potash could be further refined into pearlash by baking it in a kiln until all the carbon impurities were burned off. And for the early settlers of the New Hampshire Grants, potash was an abundant by-product of their clearing of the forests. *A Stitch In Time*, a lively work that chronicles the rise of the settlement at Townshend in Southern Vermont, describes the process as follows:

> Hardwood trees (softwoods wouldn't do) were felled, and their trunks and branches dragged into piles, set afire, and burned down to fine ashes. The ashes were shoveled into hollowed-out logs, and water was poured through them and collected as lye. The lye, which was dangerously caustic, was then carefully boiled down in enormous iron kettles over open fires. As the lye evaporated, it was chipped from the kettle and packed in leather bags for sale as potash.[7]

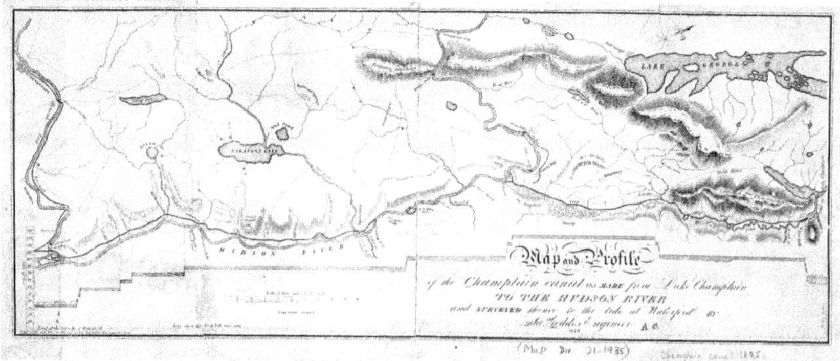

Map and profile of the Champlain Canal as made from Lake Champlain to the Hudson River and surveyed thence to the tide at Waterford

Potash kettle

According to records, potash "was mostly taken to cities outside Vermont—to Albany, to Montreal via Lake Champlain and the Richelieu River. The Brattleboro Records show that it was sent down to Connecticut . . . mostly for export."[8]

Potash transport train

The wood-fired ascent of the local economy of Brookline, where my ancestors began farming in 1788, was fast. A decade of growth that began in 1780 saw the town's population reach its peak by 1790. The hard rhythm of daily life was dryly recounted in one written history:

> The wood was cut and burned in a kiln. From the ashes, salts of lye were made, packed in wooden troughs, taken on their backs over the hill to Putney, where there was a settlement on the Connecticut River, and exchanged for the little necessaries of life.[9]

The Annals of Brattleboro 1681–1895 record that "a principal article of the produce of these towns was potash, exchanged for goods at the store—tea, coffee, tobacco, calico, and plain stuff, together with the 'mug of flip,' the common attendant of every bargain."[10]

At a time when the New England economy was primarily barter, potash and pearlash were among a few products that could be sold for cash. The market value ranged from three to five and one-half dollars per hundred pounds and peddlers would travel from village to village buying up potash made on the farms. For many of those farms, the peddlers' payment was the only cash they received all year.

It was also a way to pay for the land. "To the settlers who poured northward into Vermont after 1760, the high value of potash was good news indeed. It meant that a man, without a cent to his name, could, by hard work, eventually own a farm, for it was the general rule of thumb that the potash obtained from clearing virgin woodlands paid for the land."[11]

For settlers like my ancestor Jonathan Park, the cycle was natural. They wanted to build and farm on the land, so they had to clear the forest. Removing those trees let them produce a chemical that was in great demand. The British paid top dollar and those profits helped the first generation of settlers buy the land they cleared. It also generated enough income to enjoy life through the procurement of simple luxuries like gunpowder, salt, books, rum, and steel tools. Many families were saved from great suffering, if not from actual starvation, by selling the "salts."[12]

The clearing and farming of the land resulted in many unintended outcomes, among them soil depletion, the siltation of streams, and the loss of wildlife and fisheries. This would continue to be an issue of concern well into the future.

100 Dollars Reward

The above Reward is hereby offered for the apprehension of

Samuel Mott

a stout dark complexion person about six feet high has been engaged for some time in an illicit trade between this Government and Canada and whose violation of the laws of humanity and civil government has been instrumental in the wanton murder of two men employed in the service of the government of the United States and one private citizen, and has escaped from Justice — A Reward of Fifty Dollars each will be given for the apprehension of the following persons viz

William Noakes about 23 years of age, a stout man, about 5 feet 6 inches high, light complexion, had on a mixed home made short Coat, tow-cloth trousers and a Wool Hat, Capt Pease of common size had on a Jean coat and pantaloons about 35 years old — Slocum Clark about six feet high 22 years old had on black home made clothes and boots

Dist of Burlington
Augt 4 1808

For Jabez Penniman Collr Dist of Vermont
Nathan B Haswell, Inspector

PS. Mott and Pease have been omitted

A confidential I had employed living on the Intervale at the time of the affair of the Black Snake gave me notice, and having a good horse then at my door, I was on the ground in a few moments. I immediately seized Dean (who was afterwards hung) he appeared to have been drinking. — he was getting the better of me in the scuffle, and had drawn from his bosom a large shoe makers Knife upon which a th—Asa Rice a strong athletic man jumped upon and overpowered him. — The others could not be found. I returned to my office, and immediately issued the foregoing advertisement which [illegible] appeared in the Sentinel Augt 1808. I also sent a special messenger to Dr Penniman the Collector who approved of the course taken by me.
Nathan B Haswell

Black Snake smuggler's reward poster

The War of 1812 and the Trade Embargo

The trade in potash and pearlash was an early example to the settlers of Vermont of how events in other parts of the world could impact them. After President Thomas Jefferson imposed an embargo on trade with Britain in 1807, federal records show that the price of the two products jumped to $300 per ton. As a result, smuggling to Canada blossomed: "Nearly the whole population of the northern counties of Vermont and New York devoted their energies to the manufacture and transportation of potash to Montreal."[13]

But the spoils didn't last. "By 1807, the value of exported potash and pearlash made from wood ashes was $1,480,000. In 1810, the value was $1,579,000. In 1813, it slid down to $204,000, and after that slid to zero."[14] As is so often the case, multiple forces conspired to make New England potash obsolete, among them innovation and changing technology. In 1789, French chemist Nicolas Leblanc developed an industrial process that turned sea salt into soda ash, a method that proved faster and cheaper than the wood ash process. As the manufacture of soda ash caught on, the American woolen industry itself began to import chemically produced salts, and by the mid-1800s, industrial demand for wood ash products had practically vanished.[15, 16]

The great potash kettles around many farms and communities in Vermont lay abandoned and farmers had learned a hard lesson. Within a generation the early settlers learned that dependence on an enterprise driven by demand elsewhere, over which they had little input or control, could profoundly change their economic livelihood. These situations would exist in the future as well. With the end of the potash boom, the farmers who had cleared the land were now challenged to reinvent themselves.

CHAPTER TWO

Commercial Farming and the Development of Trade Networks

As Vermont's forests burned to woodsmoke and potash, they left behind rich, fertile soils suitable for a variety of crops and other agricultural enterprises. And as towns sprang up and their populations burgeoned, Vermont's agricultural focus shifted from subsistence to commerce: farmers supplied town stores and eventually found markets farther afield.

Farming on the western side of Vermont, in the flat and fertile Champlain Valley, specialized first. Settlers discovered that the climate and rich clay-loam soils there produced high yields of quality wheat. By 1800, the Champlain Valley was a major exporter of grain and grain products.

And the rest of Vermont was not far behind. Crockett's *History of Vermont* states, "grain, potatoes, and livestock were transported to markets in Montreal, Quebec, Troy, Albany, Hartford, Portland, New Haven, and Boston." Significant exports between 1800 and 1804 were potash, pearlash, whiskey, pork, beef, wheat flour, grain, butter, cheese, lumber, and horses.[17]

In Brookline, the town my ancestors settled in southeastern Vermont, the land had been cleared and the rich soil yielded bountiful crops for a period that lasted until around 1824. The light loamy knolls and plateaus could produce as much as 70 bushels of corn per acre without the need for costly fertilizers. White clover on which livestock grazed blanketed the hillsides in abundance.[18] Such was the image of a period of general prosperity for Vermont's early 19th century farms.

An annual commercial cycle began to emerge within the burgeoning agricultural sector. "Farmers would market wheat, butter, pork, hides and other products in winter when roads were better than in the summer. Butter was stored in cool cellars and by early winter farmers to the east of the Green Mountains became accustomed to making at least one trip to Boston. Then, having sold their produce, would return with purchases of tea, coffee, spices, white sugar, tobacco, and other articles not raised on Vermont farms."[19]

During this time and up until the railroads were established, drover drives of livestock to markets were common. In the *Atlas of Vermont* for 1808, Professor James Dean of the University of Vermont wrote, "12,000 to 15,000 head of beef cattle were driven from the state to the Boston market."[20]

These drives of lowing, honking, and bleating livestock were significant to Vermont's economic prospects:

> Prior to 1850 and the maturing of railroad transportation, southeast Vermont and southwest New Hampshire benefited from being major transit zones. Every autumn, many tens of thousands of sheep and cattle, horses and pigs, turkeys and geese would be driven to market. Many followed the Connecticut River Valley to Greenfield, Springfield, and Hartford. Even more would continue across Cheshire and Hillsborough Counties in New Hampshire to Worcester, Lowell and Boston. As many as a hundred thousand animals a year would pass through Keene, New Hampshire in herds of 200 to 400 animals. Moving ten to fifteen miles at best per day, it might take three or more weeks to make it to Brighton Market outside of Boston. Many drives also went through the Champlain Valley to New York.[21]

Supporting Industries

In tandem with the growth of towns and commercial farming, industries that supported agriculture sprang up across the state. Blacksmiths, tanneries, gristmills, carting mills, sawmills, foundries, starch mills, and other establishments all found customers among the region's growing farm settlements and contributed to the commercial development of agriculture within the state of Vermont.

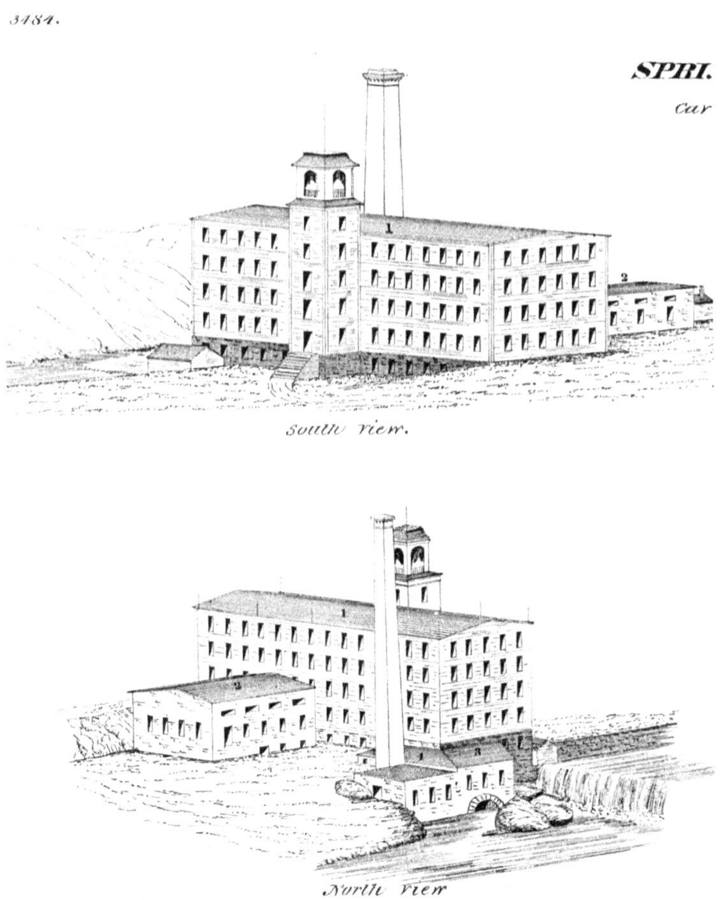

Spring Woolen Mill, Cavendish Vermont

Histories of local towns record the rise of these early industries. Water from rivers and dams was a major source of power, and so most were located close to water sources. Saw mills, dependent on water power for their operation, were among the first structures built in newly settled towns near to a stream or river. Settlers cleared forest to create farmland and turned trees into planks for housing, barns, and fences.[22]

By the 1820s nearly every settlement had at least one mill dedicated to an agrarian enterprise. For example, in Jericho, Horatio B. Barney's carding mill was built in 1819; Shelburne Falls, with durable waterpower, had one flour mill, one sawmill, one shingle mill, and a blacksmith shop.[23] Brookline, the town I grew up in, had three sawmills, two grist mills and two tanneries along with three stores, two hotels, two blacksmith shops, a potash-making facility, doctor, and councilor of law.[24]

Transportation Networks

An essential part of commercial success for any farmer is the ability to get goods to market. The development of transportation networks, on both land and water, played a key role in commerce at the turn of the nineteenth century.

Turnpikes

Road building is said to have begun in the late 1700s with private turnpikes chartered by the Vermont legislature. Among the first was the Windham Turnpike Company, which was incorporated in 1799 and built a road for travel between Brattleboro and Bennington. The company was permitted to erect five tollgates.[25]

The Town of Poultney is another example of a settlement whose fortunes rose with the growth of transportation networks. Poultney Village's growth began as a function of geography: its location, at the halfway point in the two-day journey between Burlington to the north and the Hudson River near Albany to the south, proved to be a welcome break in a long journey. As early as 1800, an inn and tavern operated at the crossroads where passengers could rest overnight, and stagecoaches would stop to change horses.

In 1806 some enterprising investors saw an opportunity and formed the Poultney Turnpike Company to create a toll road. One-hundred-man labor parties and ox-drawn plows smoothed the rough and twisting trail. At the end of one fourth of July work party, the townspeople celebrated their emerging road and the optimism that it conveyed with a community dinner and sixteen toasts—among them "to the Patriotic Diggers" and "to the Ladies Who Got the Meal."[26]

By 1811, the new, privately owned Poultney Turnpike (now Route 30) was completed, connecting the town to other turnpikes and toll roads. Until the canals and then the railroads were built, this turnpike was the best route for stagecoaches and wagons, which brought regular mail to the frontier. Local farmers could transport their produce to markets in Albany. Cattle prodders, herding their stock to the markets of Boston, would pause at the town for the night.

Tollgates soon dotted the Turnpike and while the 10-cent toll was collected from those passing through, locals living within 8 miles had their tolls waived. This practice raised some controversy as everyone was soon claiming they lived within those eight miles. Up the slope, there was often a detour over rougher terrain, what was then called a "shun-pike," that allowed travelers to skip out on the toll. During this turnpike era, Poultney farmers relied on their cash crops of grain and dairy. Records suggest that one early settler, William Ward, hauled "1,714 pounds of cheese and whiskey" to market in a single shipment.[27]

The 10-cent toll was only one cost of shipping. In addition was added the cost of the wagon, the draft horses, and labor. For instance, when Ward hauled his goods along the turnpikes some eighty miles to the port near Albany, his account books noted that shipping costs accounted for 37 percent of his salt and 23 percent of his whisky.[28]

The cost of maintaining and staffing the turnpikes was not cheap. While the tolls added expense to the many costs of transportation, one toll syndicate reported an annual profit of only $30. And so, while the Poultney Turnpike had secured the village's role as a prosperous transportation center from the 1800s into the 1840s, in 1823 the completion of the Champlain Canal substantially reduced the Turnpike profits. In 1831 the Poultney Turnpike became a public highway.[29]

These turnpikes became the spokes that connected an increasingly interdependent agricultural economy. Their spread eased the way for stagecoaches that took travelers and commerce to distant markets. In 1801 a single stagecoach made weekly trips up and down the Connecticut Valley; another made the trip to and from Boston each week. By 1807 three weekly stages passed through Bellows Falls between Boston and Hanover, NH. In 1814, a regular four-horse coach was put on the route between Burlington and Boston.[30]

Lakes and Rivers

Lake Champlain and the Richelieu and St. Lawrence Rivers were used as key routes by Vermont colonists for trade with Canada for many years. In his must-read article "Jay's Treaty: The Transformation of Lake Champlain Commerce," H. Nicholas Muller explains that in the late 1790s:

> Champlain Valley farmers and merchants sent produce to markets as far away as Troy and Albany, Portland, Boston, Hartford, New Haven, and New York. But the majority of their surplus production of wheat, oats, hops, corn, rye, pease, varieties of seeds, cheese, butter, honey, cattle, oxen, horse, salt beef, and salt pork went to Canada.[31]

Muller notes that "the *Montreal Gazette* regularly carried advertisements for cheese, honey, beeswax, sole leather, and corn from the Champlain basin. D. A. Grout proudly announced that he used 'Lake Champlain flour' in his Québec bakehouse."[32]

Until the mid-1790s, most of this commerce had occurred using great rafts constructed on the lake ice in winter and then floated north to Quebec City in the spring. It was an arduous journey that included a set of rapids that could only be navigated during the spring floods. That meant all the rafts arrived together, flooding the market and yielding poor profits for the Vermont merchants.

When the Jay Treaty took effect in 1796, however, new protections around commerce between the U.S. and Britain led to a new flourishing of regional trade. While much Vermont timber still traveled to Quebec City, potash and other goods increasingly traveled to the much-closer city of Montreal, heralding "an era of prosperity into the commerce of the Champlain-Richelieu route."[33]

The steamboat Vermont *in dry dock*

The Jay Treaty period saw Burlington's transformation into a significant economic center. In 1792, Burlington was largely a forest. There were no wharves, and goods brought in sloops were landed in scows, with the exception of casks of liquor and molasses, which were floated ashore. In a fortuitous convergence of innovation and circumstance, the passage of the Jay Treaty coincided with a new era of lake vessels. Muller documents that thirty-one commercial shipping vessels went into service between 1776 and 1812, including the second steamboat in the U.S., the 120-foot *Vermont*.[34]

Trade with Canada diminished after the War of 1812, when post-war tariffs disincentivized trade with Britain, forest depletion led to the end of the rafting tradition, and new canal systems opened up easier access to markets to the south.

Canals

The first canal system in the United States was in Bellows Falls, Vermont with the Connecticut River being the first major waterway in the country improved for travel by 1810. In Bellows Falls a canal was begun in 1792 with English capital.[35] It is said that by means of flat-bottomed boats on this canal, a large freight business was done for many years between Hartford, Connecticut, and Bellows Falls, Vermont. These boats were 72 feet long and 11½ feet wide and when loaded carried 30 tons and had a draw of 2–3 feet of water. It took approximately three days to get to Hartford.[36]

The Annals of Brattleboro, 1681–1895, record that the firm name of Holbrook & Porter of Brattleboro started the first flat-bottomed boats on the Connecticut River between the town and Hartford, and for many years these boats were the principal means of exchanging heavy freight with seaboard. The firm also owned the *Highlander*, a flatboat that would carry twenty-four tons and the largest on the river. Holbrook & Porter also built a slaughterhouse on the island across the river, where large quantities of beef, pork, hams, and tongues were cured for the West Indian Market.[37] Other boats operated on the river all the way from Wells River.

The trip from Wells River to Hartford and the return took about twenty-five days. The items brought back included iron products, salt, rum, sugar, molasses, and other heavy articles. Freight charges were significant. Perhaps the most significant canal for Vermont's growing agricultural economy was the Champlain Canal. Constructed simultaneously with the Erie Canal, the shorter Champlain Canal opened two years earlier, in 1823, and is heralded as bringing the end of the Champlain Valley's isolation and its entry into the national economy.

The opening of the Champlain Canal profoundly shaped the economic development of the Champlain Valley. Support for the canal's construction had come from businesses that saw its value, including lumber businesses along the lake, the iron mining industry on the New York shore, and Vermont marble cutters. The sloop *Gleaner*, built at St. Albans, Vermont was the first vessel to complete a voyage through the new canal from Lake Champlain. *The Woodstock Observer* noted that "the *Gleaner* has on board 1,000 bushels of wheat and 35 barrels of potash." It goes on to say, "While cargoes of iron ore and other natural resources generated much of the canal traffic from Lake Champlain, shipments of butter and cheese increased five-fold and wool fifty times."[38] A decade after opening, in 1833, 232 canal boats were registered at the ports of

Lake Champlain or along the Champlain Canal; in another ten years the number of canal boats had almost doubled to an estimated 450.

The Albany Basin of the Erie and Champlain Canals

Top among the canal's immediate benefits, agricultural surpluses of bountiful Vermont products—apples, potatoes, grain, butter, cheese— were shipped quickly and inexpensively to urban centers along the Eastern Seaboard. And the Canal provided Vermonters and northeastern New Yorkers with raw materials and manufactured goods that had once been costly to ship overland or import from Canada. As transportation networks proliferated, Vermont's agricultural economy continued to orient production toward regional export markets. In an article, "Local History and the Vermont Borderlands, 1790–1820," the author, based on her extensive research of Chittenden County and its agriculture around the period of 1819, found that:

> Although farmers faced transport difficulties, wheat rapidly became "Vermont's cash crop" by the turn of the century. The building of the Champlain Canal in 1823, which gave Lake Champlain traffic access to the Hudson River, offered the promise of an even more profitable market for wheat. However, the canal would ultimately

shift agricultural production in directions different to those found during the region's formative years.[39]

The Erie Canal and Midwestern Competition

While the Champlain Canal gave western Vermont easy access to big-city markets, its effect was soon overshadowed by the 363-mile Erie Canal. It began just 200 years ago, on July 4th, 1817 when the beginning of a 40-ft. wide and 4-ft. deep canal was begun to connect the Hudson River at Rome, New York to the Great Lakes, 363 miles to the east. The canal was completed eight years and four months later at a cost of 7.1 million dollars. Tolls paid off its construction costs within eight years.

It was not a new idea, connecting the West to the East; the thought had been floating around since the 1780s. However, federal funding for it had been rejected by President Thomas Jefferson, who is said to have stated that "talk of a canal 350 miles through the wilderness is a little short of madness."[40] It took the determination of DeWitt Clinton, Governor of New York, and the New York legislature to make it a reality. Detractors (and there were many) called it "Clinton's big ditch." It was an immediate success when it opened on October 26, 1825.

The canal transformed North America and was soon called the greatest engineering feat of 19th century America. Some even marveled when it was completed that it was The Eighth Wonder of the World. It was the longest artificial waterway and the greatest public works project of its time in North America. How it transformed agriculture, commerce, and geography in America was its greatest achievement.

The canal quickly positioned New York City as a leading economic and commercial city with the most important seaport in North America. The port at New York, now connected via the Hudson River to the western frontier, became a strategic commercial center. The city's population quadrupled between 1820 and 1850 and a great many more passed through it as they embarked on the journey West.

Many thoughtful historians have concluded that the opening of the Erie Canal resulted in the demise of New England agriculture, opening Eastern markets to inexpensive Western goods. Farmers, loggers, miners, and manufacturers now had quick access to the growing markets of the

East. For example, a ton of wheat from the Midwest to the Northeast before the Erie Canal cost $100 per ton, and only about fourteen thousand bushels were shipped east. After the Canal, it cost $10 per ton to ship a product and it took one-third of the time. In 1840, for example, about eight million bushels of wheat were shipped East from the Midwest. The East began to rely on the midwest for food and other products, and New York City became the international gateway. The Erie Canal made the West accessible and valuable, unlocking the floodgates to western settlement.

Dr. Ann Green, a professor of history at the University of Pennsylvania, has observed that:

> The decline of the agricultural society in Connecticut and the rest of New England is due in part to the way the Erie Canal connected the inexpensive lands of the Midwest with the most densely populated regions of the country. While it allowed for bulky materials like grain, lumber, and rock to be imported easily from other areas of the country, it also provided a "route" for immigrants to head west. People had been trying to farm New England for 300 years, but not always in a kind fashion. There was soil exhaustion, and better, cheaper land out West. It becomes a real route for immigration.[41]

What has become known as a "Canal-building mania" lasted a decade or so after the completion of the Erie, with some 3000 miles of waterways constructed by 1840, including the Chambly Canal, which eased the passage along the Richelieu and Saint Lawrence trade route to the north. In the 1820s, plans were discussed for a second major canal in Vermont—the Onion River Canal—connecting the Connecticut River to Lake Champlain in Vermont.[42, 43]

Innovation in transportation was again coming to the region, inaugurating a new era of disruption. In the same way that canals would impact toll roads and stagecoaches, railroads constructed after the 1840s would lead to the economic demise of the canal system and any plans to expand or create new canals. Although at first canal shipping was protected by a law that prohibited the carrying of freight on the railroad during the navigation season,[44] railroads were faster, cheaper, and did not freeze over in the winter, and these advantages soon carried the day.

CHAPTER THREE

The Sheep Craze

BY THE 1820S, Vermont's grain business was in trouble. Decades of continuous cropping had exhausted the soils, leading to declining yields. In the 1830s, crops were devastated two years in a row by a wheat midge epidemic, a fly outbreak during which the larvae attack the spring wheat kernel, destroying harvests. And, after the completion of the Erie Canal in 1825, Vermont faced increasing competition from midwestern grain growers. For Vermont farmers, however, the next great agricultural opportunity was on the scene: sheep.

The sheep industry transformed Vermont and New England's landscape in the 1800s. First introduced from Spain in the early years of the century, Vermont's Merino sheep grazed on the hills and in the valleys and became known worldwide for their fine wool. By 1840, Vermont boasted 1.6 million sheep (the state's human population at the time was about 300,000). Today the hills of Vermont are dotted with cellar holes and stone walls that date back to this thriving period, and many woolen mill buildings constructed during this time still exist throughout the region. These mills played an important role in the woolen industry during the years between 1810 and 1870. It was here that the wool was processed into finished goods.

Herman Brown and his sheep, East Dover, Vermont

From Spain to Vermont

William Jarvis is the most well-known importer and promoter of Merino sheep, but he was not the first. That distinction goes to David Humphreys, said to be one of the most accomplished Connecticut men of the early republic. He was an aide-de-camp to General George Washington,[45] and then served as foreign minister, first to Portugal (1791–1796) and then to Spain (1796–1801), under the presidencies of George Washington and John Adams.

Humphreys was introduced to the Merino breed during his time in Spain. Merinos had been bred for their fine fleece and were sheep of the hills. While the export of this breed was prohibited by the Spanish authorities, Humphreys took advantage of his connections and purchased one hundred sheep (seventy-five ewes and twenty-five rams) and shipped them to his home in Derby, Connecticut, as well as to a farm in Westminster, Vermont. This initial and fortuitous experience positioned Humphreys to become the first successful

Portrait of David Humphreys

importer of Merino sheep into the United States. As word spread about the quality and quantity of the fleece, offers came pouring in for the sheep, at much higher prices than he had paid. He established the first large woolen mill in the United States in 1806, in what was then known as Humphreysville, now Seymour, Connecticut.[46] Humphreys' success with his sheep transformed agriculture in Connecticut and New England and is said to have encouraged men to follow his example and build woolen mills.

Jarvis the Merino Evangelist

William Jarvis has been called an "evangelist" for the Merino sheep, or some might say he was to the nascent sheep industry what Ben Cohen and Jerry Greenfield are to ice cream. His history, both as consul to Portugal and eventually as a resident of Weathersfield, Vermont is well documented. The son of a prominent Boston family, Jarvis had an early business failure, but with the help of his father, he reestablished himself. He went on to create and run a successful international trading firm, and in this capacity, he became very well connected with government officials

Portrait of William Jarvis

and business leaders throughout Europe. Because of these connections, President Jefferson appointed him consul to Portugal.[47]

For many years, Merinos had been protected by Spain from export as a way to sustain the price of fine wool. However, with the invasion of Spain by Napoleon, there was concern about the plight of the breed. Jarvis took advantage of this political and military unrest and used his connections to ship some of these prized animals to the United States in 1809. While he was not the first to do so, he was one of the first to become an advocate for their advancement in the U.S. According to information published in 1879 by the Vermont Merino Sheep Breeders Association, some 15,767 Merino sheep arrived throughout the East Coast from

Spain in 1810 and 1811. Boston received twenty-nine vessels carrying a total of 2,048 sheep; New York received 52 vessels totaling 9,349 sheep; Philadelphia received four vessels totaling 389 sheep; and other ships went to Norfolk, Virginia; New Haven, Connecticut; Portland, Maine; and Providence, Rhode Island.[48] (When Jarvis shipped the sheep, he sent some as a gift to Jefferson.[49])

The Merino Comes to Vermont

As the story of Merinos in America is told, Jarvis was looking for a location in Virginia to bring his sheep. However, an uncle and a cousin living in Claremont, New Hampshire suggested a farm across the river in Weathersfield, Vermont which Jarvis purchased upon his return from Spain.[50] The location proved ideal for these sheep: much of the land had been stripped of trees for potash, lumber, and firewood by an earlier generation of settlers and grass now covered the hills and valleys. Sheep thrived on the grass growing in poor, rocky soils.

Vermont Merino farm of William Jarvis

Jarvis settled his sheep in Weathersfield, along with shepherds, dogs, and other animals. He purchased and cleared additional acreage around this farm and soon became known as a "zealot" for the advancement of the Merino sheep breed in the United States. While Vermont had sheep before this time, and woolen mills too, the wool was not the quality of the Merino. Jarvis helped fuel the supply by lending money to farmers interested in establishing flocks and providing technical assistance. The bloodline from his flock became the foundation of the Vermont Merinos. In addition to raising the sheep, and distributing them to his fellow Vermonters, he traveled around the country speaking to the merits of the Merinos and their wool. He even employed a network of merchants for selling wool, and became a part owner and investor in a textile mill in Quechee, Vermont.

By the first half of 1830s, it was said that Vermont farmers were selling their cows to make room for more sheep. In a pattern that would become common to Vermont, many small farms were consolidated during this period into larger ones. Sensing an opportunity to make quick cash and try their hand at fortune elsewhere, some farmers sold their farms and moved West, for "it paid the well-to-do to buy up the small places, use the barns for sheep folds, and let the houses fall into the cellars."[51]

By 1840, Vermont was the sheep capital of the world. Many towns in Vermont had at least 1,000 sheep, according to records, and Addison County had the greatest number: the Town of Shoreham alone was home to 40,000 sheep. It is said, "it was the Vermont soil, Vermont climate, and the Yankee skill" that made the state an ideal place for this industry to thrive.[52]

The Rise and Fall of Vermont's Wool Industry

Prior to Jefferson's Embargo Act of 1807, fine woven wool came from England. The embargo, and then the War of 1812, blocked imports and paralyzed trade. As Merino sheep had been imported by then to Vermont and the northeast, the raising of Merino sheep for wool expanded quickly. Early American mills needed product and the fine fleece of the domestic Merinos was in ever greater demand. Enthusiastic about the prospects of a nascent textile industry in the United States, Jefferson wrote to his friend the Marquis de Lafayette:

> Our embargo . . . has produced one very happy and
> permanent effect. It has set us on domestic manufacturing
> and will, I verily believe, reduce our future demands on

England fleece in half. We are all eager to get into the
Merino race of sheep.[53]

This period of unrest with Britain fueled a manufacturing
independence streak in the United States. When the war ended with the
Treaty of Ghent in 1814, British manufactured goods, including cotton
and woolen goods, once again flooded the U.S. markets. This time they
faced an unprecedented level of domestic competition.

During the years after the war Jarvis became a power in Vermont
politics.[54] It is said that he spent ten thousand dollars advocating publicly
and privately for protective tariffs on imported wool.[55] With significant
pressure from the Vermont delegation and with the aid of Jarvis's pro-
tariff pamphlets addressed to high-powered friends, Congress eventually
passed a high tariff on imported wool in 1824. It is said that during
this time, "that manufacturers went from county to county offering large
prices for fine wool." And not everyone was pleased by these protective
import taxes. A subsequent tariff, the Tariff of 1828, was called the "tariff
of abominations" by opponents in the South who depended on the
English demand for cotton and increased the cost of British textiles. They
felt that the embargo benefited the industrial north, and the political
backlash led to a gradual repeal of tariffs during the 1830s and 1840s.

After the opening of the Erie Canal in 1825, Vermont wool producers
also faced increasing competition from midwestern sheep farmers. It
cost $1–$2 per head to produce sheep in Vermont, compared to as little
as 25 cents per head in the Midwest. The Erie Canal—and, later, the
railroad—could carry midwestern wool to be purchased by the mills in
Massachusetts and New York at prices far below what New England
farmers would accept.[56]

Also, after the repeal of the tariffs, no system of small flocks like
Vermont's could compete with the flocks in Australia and Argentina,
which commonly stood at anywhere from 100,000 to 400,000 sheep. In
response to these economic pressures, Vermont sheep farmers found a
new way to earn their livelihoods: breeding.

In *They Lit Their Cigars with Five Dollar Bills: The History of the
Merino Sheep Industry in Addison County*, Betty Jane Belanus covers the
Merino sheep period and those involved.[57] As the wheat trade declined,

many Addison County farmers had become Merino sheep owners, and one, Edwin Hammond of Middlebury, is said to have established perhaps the most famous flock of Merinos in history. Belanus goes on to recount that after 1850 the number of sheep in Addison County began to decrease. Enterprising breeders saw that the next phase in the industry lay in the exportation of fine Addison County Merinos to points west. Thus the Merino began the next stage of its migration from Spain, out from Vermont to the vast and rolling grasslands of the West.

An Addison County report of the period shows that as early as 1843 local Merino men found they could make substantial profits by selling their sheep outside the County. Therefore more breeders were getting into the export business. The sheep, driven to Whitehall, New York or transported there by ferry from points in Addison County such as Frost's Ferry in Bridport or Larrabee's Point in Shoreham, were shipped by canal to their destinations. To get to points farther west, the sheep were loaded on steamers from Buffalo.

Pure bred Merino sheep

By 1860 Addison County breeders of Merinos were among the best stock-breeders in the nation. During this time, the size of a good sheep farm in the County was from 250–500 acres and tells a complex story of prosperity, consolidation, and migration among sheep farmers. "The business of grazing requires large farms to satisfy the ambition of the enterprising," an Addison County report of the time relates. "And the large profits have enabled the wealthier to crowd out the smaller landowners and send them to the West." The report goes on to make a grim and often repeated conclusion, that "The result has been that in several of the principal agricultural towns, the number of the farmers, and of course the population, has considerably diminished."[58]

The Civil War, however, was the real Golden Age of Vermont Merino breeding. The period between 1863 and 1867 brought more money to Addison County Merino breeders than any other ten-year period, as the war stimulated the wool industry by simultaneously preventing trade in cotton from the South and upping demand for clothing and blankets. The great wool growers of the West came to Vermont where they paid premium prices for Merino rams. Ram prices were said to be as high as $3,500 and as a result many beautiful houses, barns, and outbuildings were built with the proceeds.

As a further inducement to the interest in the Vermont Merino, at the International Exhibition in Hamburg, Germany in 1863, a Vermont Merino took two first prizes for having the heaviest fleece and longest wool of any other sheep exhibited in its class. These sheep, according to the breeder George Campbell, were all descendants of the importations of Jarvis and Humphrey.

George Campbell of West Westminster, Vermont, was the only American who dared to take livestock across the Atlantic and the German oceans, and the results of his skillful American breeding has been compared with those of European breeders. Mr. Campbell was rewarded for the risk that he took. It is said that no greater surprise could have been created on the continent of Europe than was awakened by the announcement that his American sheep had taken two first prizes in the class of Merinos, one for the length of staple, and the other for the weight of the fleece. In all George had brought 12 sheep to the fair of 1863, competing against Europe's finest, including some from the Royal French flock.[59]

As a result of that success, it soon became the common opinion that America not only had the most valuable Merinos on the exhibition grounds but the most valuable in Europe.[60]

Flush with success, Merino sheep breeders of Addison County saw this as the time to preserve the reputation of Vermont Merinos, and a group formed the Vermont Merino Sheep Breeders Association.

Probably one of the better summaries of the "boom and bust" nature of the agricultural economics of this period is from this association in 1879:

> No farm stock except Merino sheep has been affected by such extraordinary seasons of favor, amounting to mania, when prices have been enhanced to such extraordinary fictitious values when large numbers without qualifications or due consideration have embarked in the business of breeding them until by the action of some unfriendly legislation it would immediately follow depressing prices…until…flocks of Merinos…crushed out and threatened with annihilation.[61]

At a later period, the report goes on to indicate that at the industry's height in 1881, 6,777 sheep were shipped by rail from Middlebury to the West. This export is said to have then decreased after Western wool growers began to feel the impact of additional tariff reductions in 1883.

The Merino sheep period forever changed Vermont's landscape, its culture, and its agricultural and manufacturing industry. And then, in the late 1880s, the sheep industry in Vermont had become unprofitable and Vermont's position as a leading producer of some of the finest Merino wool came to an end. This was due to many factors including tariff protection changes, Western and international competition, and the cost of producing sheep on smaller farms and acreage.

The foundation for the switch from sheep raising to dairying as Vermont's main industry was laid during this period, the next phase of commercial farming in the state. But it would still take some time before the dairy sector would reach full bloom.

Effect on the Landscape

Interestingly, many were concerned at the time with the impact that the sheep were having on the landscape.[62] It is stated that George Perkins Marsh, a respected Vermont lawyer and early conservationist, knew that Vermonters had "rushed to breed Merino sheep, which like an invasive species, crowded practically every other agricultural animal and activity out of its way. Deforestation, overgrazing, cycles of flood and drought, not to mention the hollowing out of Vermont's farms and towns, ensued."[63] Merino sheep could have turned the Champlain Valley and the eastern slopes of the Adirondacks into a desert.

Adaption to Change and Diversity in Vermont Farming

A quick survey of Vermont's agricultural economy in 1850 is recorded in Crockett's *History of Vermont,* which shows that:

> Vermont had 29,763 farms with an average value per acre of $19.09, or in today's dollars, approximately $550.00 per acre. In the State, there were 146,128 milch cows [cows kept for milking], 154,143 horses, 1,014,122 sheep, and 66,296 swine. During this time, the following agricultural products were produced in the state: 12 million pounds of butter; 9 million pounds of cheese; 3.4 million pounds of wool. Other products included: 2 million bushels of corn; ½ million bushels of wheat; 2 million bushels of oats; 42 thousand bushels of barley; 176,000 bushels of rye; 209,000 bushels of buckwheat; 105,000 bushels of field beans; 5 million bushels of potatoes; 866,000 tons of hay; $315 worth of orchard products; 20 thousand pounds of flax; 288,000 pounds of hops; 260 pounds of silk in cocoons; 6 million pounds of maple sugar; 5.697 gallons of maple syrup; and 249,000 pounds of honey. In the Fourth Report of the State Board of Agriculture in 1877, it is stated "that 90% of what is consumed is raised in the State of Vermont. The State exports 50% of its oats, 80% of its potatoes, 2/3s of its butter, but imports 40% of its flour and 50% of its meat.[64]

In earlier times, flour in the state had been made exclusively from Vermont grains. Now having seen the loss of being the major grain-producing region of the Northeast, they were not only not exporting grains but were having to import much of what they used. For example, it is stated, "by 1826 the State was importing 15,000 barrels of flour per year." Vermont farmers had also seen the dire economic realities as western beef and wool, as well as grain, forced a change in the production in Vermont of these commodities to other products of value such as butter and cheese from the dairy cows.

Nevertheless, even during the height of Vermont's sheep mania, diversified farming remained common. One can find examples of these diversified products on Vermont family farms in the diary of Roxanna Watts of Peacham, Vermont. Her diary from the year 1866 (see *Roxana's Children*) records the many seasonal activities of a farm typical in its time:

> Sugaring in the spring; planting oats, wheat, potatoes, beans in May; shearing sheep and "drawing muck"— spreading of manure in June; harvesting hay in July and August and cutting oats and wheat; In September cutting corn, picking apples, and marketing sheep and lambs. In October and November, husked corn, plowed and picked, and drew stones. All this in addition to the daily chores.[65]

This diversity of production in Vermont agriculture illustrates that farmers have long been aware that their existence depended upon their ability to adapt to the pressures of changing economic times. The demise of the Merino sheep industry and before that wheat in the Champlain Valley and the potash trade are key examples of how events and innovation in policies, markets, technologies, and transportation can change agriculture in a state and region.

Although a key economic focus during the early and mid-1800s was on Merino sheep, other changes were taking place as well. These include:

- Large-scale migration from Vermont had begun by 1810, many of these migrants joining the movement West. A number of events spurred this Westward tide including the ability of farmers to sell their properties and move toward the frontier where their money could buy larger properties for lesser prices. It was not just farmers moving West: "The highways seem to have been dotted with Vermont carpenters, blacksmiths, shoemakers, printers, masons, coopers and the like."[66]

- The Vermont legislature passed an act in 1835 to encourage the growing of silk. The State Treasurer was authorized to give a bounty of 10 cents for each pound of cocoons cultivated in Vermont above anything "raised or grown" elsewhere. Among the advantages of "sericulture" were the modest resources required and that its cultivation readily lent itself to child labor. Some, but very little, was grown in the years 1835 through 1850.[67] In the end, the severe Vermont winters were said to kill the planting of mulberry trees and those Vermont farmers who were engaged in this type of agriculture experiment abandoned the work.[68]

- In 1829 the Fairbanks brothers, known for their manufacture of cast-iron wares, added a new line of business, the processing of hemp. Used in the making of sails and rigging on ships in coastal cities, Vermont's production expanded in the 1820s. Due to inaccurate methods to weigh the product, the brothers invented the platform scale, which became the renowned business which built their legacy.[69]

- Intoxicating liquors were an issue during the early part of the 1800s, including cider, brandy, and corn and rye whiskies. In 1810 alone there were 125 distilleries in the State making 173,000 gallons of apple brandy (U.S. Census of 1810). At the height of production there were said to be two hundred distilleries in the State of Vermont with many towns having one or more. This period came to an end with the Temperance movement and legislation in 1852 that prohibited the manufacture and sale of intoxicating liquor as a beverage but permitted its use "for sacramental purposes."[70]

- Horse raising and trade were important agricultural activities in the early years according to records. For example, "Randolph and Royalton furnished many to export and to the driving-horse trade. The cheaper grades are being sold as streetcar horses. Mule colts were also raised for the West Indies sugar trade."[71]

- Hops were an important crop in the 1800s as well. According to data, by 1850 Vermont was second to New York in production. That represented 8 percent of U.S. production. Eventually this industry, due to economics, moved westward as well.[72]

- The legislature of 1779 required each town to care for the poor, and this was based upon the "poor laws" of England. Poor farms were established throughout Vermont. The intent was for these to become self-sufficient from crops sold as income, with labor coming from those sent there as being poor and paupers. (See "Caring for the Poor," *In Times Past*, March 25, 2009, larrycoffin.blogspot.com/2009/03/caring-for-poor.html.) The establishment of these farms also demonstrated the importance of agriculture to local communities. The last poor farm closed in 1968. Vermont's Social Welfare Act of 1967 formally removed from the towns both the right to operate a poor farm and the legal responsibility for the care of the poor.[73]

CHAPTER FOUR

Commercial Butter and Cheese Production

WHILE THE WOOL INDUSTRY SHRANK from midwestern competition and some sheep farmers turned to breeding to survive, another industry slowly gained footing in Vermont. Starting around 1840, dairying, and butter making specifically, began a transition from incidental small-farm production to major commercial product. Franklin County was on the leading edge of this industry, committing to milk cows around 1850.

A nascent railroad system was essential to the county's dairying success. The Central Vermont Railroad, completed in 1850, was headquartered in Saint Albans where it proved pivotal to the region's access to more distant markets.

A paper read before the Vermont Board of Agriculture in 1872 by Dr. R. R. Sherman of St. Albans discusses the history of the St. Albans dairy market in detail. According to Dr. Sherman, before 1840 Montreal was almost the only market farmers of Northern Vermont could use to sell their surplus products. He relates that, "When St. Lawrence was frozen, the farmers loaded into their double sleighs their dressed hogs, butter, and skim-milk cheese, and started for Montreal." About 1840 the tide began to change and farm products started to float the other way. Around that time, butter and cheese became more demanded as manufacturing districts sprang up throughout New England and the Middle States.

Buyers, Dr. Sherman claimed, went through Franklin County and bought the butter and cheese to be delivered at St. Albans Bay.[74]

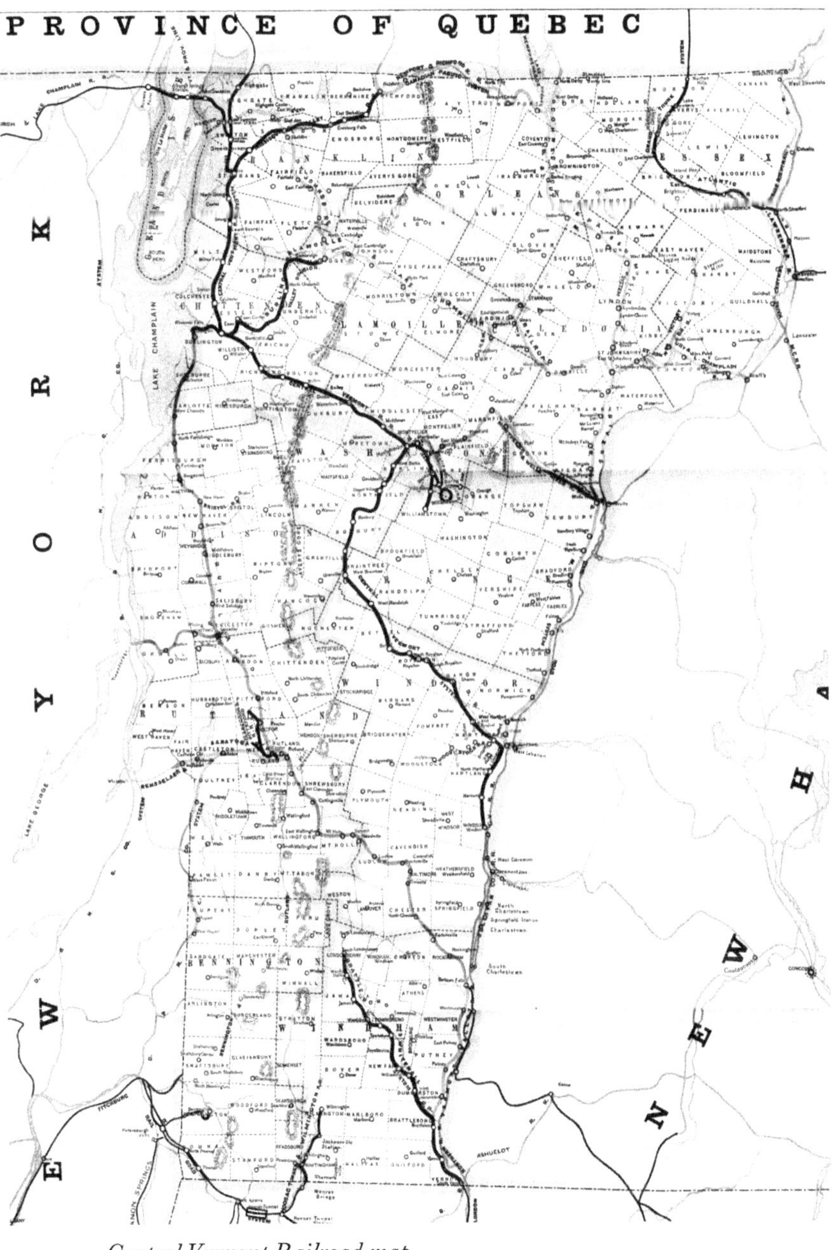

Central Vermont Railroad map

With the completion of the Central Vermont Railroad, however, major cities such as Boston and New York were now only a few hours away. This opened new dairy markets for products with a short shelf-life. A significant improvement for this shipment was the development of refrigerated rail cars by Jonas Wilder of Rouses Point, NY, who lined a 36-foot wooden boxcar and poured ice between the inner and outer walls. Wilder became manager of the Central Vermont Railroad there and put into service the first refrigerated railcar in 1851. His cooling method meant that dairy items, meat, vegetables, and fruits could be packed fresh and shipped long distances without spoilage.[75]

By 1854 the Central Vermont Railroad had started to run a refrigerated butter train weekly from St. Albans to Boston. Tuesday was said to be market day and the streets thronged with as many as 300 wagon teams bringing products from throughout the county to the cold storage building by the railroad tracks. The building also housed meeting rooms where buyers from around the region conducted their business.

Thirty years later, a thriving dairy and produce market facilitated by the train network resulted in a quarter of the butter produced in the state coming from Franklin County. Showing just how important the trains were to Franklin County trade, Col. Clarke of St. Albans "regarded Franklin's preeminence in butter as mainly due to the extra inducements in freight charges offered by the Railroad to shippers from that point, the terms being better than even from some points not over fifty miles from Boston." He continued:

> Barre is the best farming town in Vermont, having the best and least wasteland, and Montpelier might have as good a butter market as St. Albans with the same facilities for shipping. The other markets are gaining, especially Richmond and Vergennes, and now the Rutland road is controlled by the Central, better facilities will be given along its line.[76]

The combined circumstances of having some of the best butter in the Northeast along with ready access to the market created conditions where attempts to control supply and increase profits would be inevitable.

One such effort was led by B. F. Rugg and took place through the year in 1856. Rugg, a prominent dealer in butter in Franklin County and across the state, developed a plan to control the butter supply to the Boston market. He also had the brains, energy, confidence, contacts, and financial resources to do so. He set about buying butter in the spring when prices were low and quietly storing it in local cellars. He continued this practice through July and August, sending only small supplies to the market each week to avoid detection for withholding it. He continued to buy and hold the product until the price was at a level where he could make a substantial profit. As peak production ended and the supply fell, Rugg found the demand in the Boston market to be so great that eventually, they would agree to his price. The gain of Rugg's adventure in controlling the supply that year amounted to $18,000, or about $531,670 in today's dollar value. His attempt to repeat his scheme the following year failed.[77]

In the first decades of the industry, production still took place on farms. Farmers had always made butter and cheese for their own consumption and to barter locally, and these skills were passed down from one generation to the next. "The herds [are] milked in the open yard: the curds worked in tubs and log presses. Everything is done by guess, with no order, system, or science."[78]

The women of the farm were essential to this process, as related in the First Annual Report of the State Board of Agriculture in 1872:

> There are several essential elements necessary to the making of good butter to include good cows, good feed, good salt, a good churn, and a good woman, and some say that the possession of the last would ensure the first four.[79]

As the demand for butter continued to increase, farmers often responded to the opportunity more quickly than some thought they should, and not with the best cattle. As is so often the case in markets prone to speculative forces, some came to claim that if one-half as much thought were given to the dairy business as was given to sheep raising, dairy production would double. Others contended that at least one-fourth of the cows used in milking were worthless, and everyone went into business haphazard. Everything in the shape of a cow was brought into dairy and without thought or care to milk production with the animal.[80]

Tied to the Wrong Cow

"Tied to the Wrong Cow" cartoon

One individual quoted in the Fourth Report of the State Board of Agriculture in 1877 observed that "Butter making is a fine art. There are probably more good poets, painters, and sculptors than first-class butter makers."[81] Another said, "Poor butter is an abomination; to eat it is to degrade the physical, intellectual, and moral nature of man; to furnish it for the table a great wrong; to make it may not be the unpardonable sin, but it is a fault exceedingly difficult to forgive or forget."[82]

Gradually attempts were made to increase the quality of local butter. In 1870 the Vermont Dairymen's Association was formed, one of the first boards of its kind in the United States.[83] One of their initiatives was to bring better cattle genetics into milk production on the farm. Frederick Billings imported cattle from the Isle of Jersey in 1871 to his farm in Woodstock, Vermont.[84] The Jersey breed soon became the dominant breed in Vermont for butter and cheese production.[85]

The Jersey Cow: "The Butter Queen"

Growth of Local Creameries

As demand grew and observers witnessed the export of Vermont's fine cream and butter to larger markets, creameries sprang up in many towns and communities around the state.[86] In 1887, M. W. Davis, a member of the State Board of Agriculture from Westminster, Vermont, stated at a regional meeting of the Board (Shelburne Institute) that "sheep raising in Vermont has gone to the wall. What, then, is our specialty? No industry presents itself which is as encouraging as dairy. If this is our principal industry, why not pursue it intelligently? The inventor has come to your aid. Throw down the walls of prejudice and go into cooperative creameries."[87] He went on to elaborate at other meetings of the State Board of Agriculture across the state on the subject as a member of the Board (Manchester Institute), saying that "Vermont has the soil, climate, water and grasses that peculiarly adapt it to the production of the best butter, and that it can be made profitably, even with Western competition, if the right course is pursued."[88]

Among the first to begin capturing more of milk's value in the state were Richmond Creamery, founded in 1880 and employing up to 200 people at its height, and North River Creamery in Jacksonville, which started in 1886.[89] Products were distributed throughout New England.

Vermont's local historical societies and documents found elsewhere give information on many of these creameries. For example, Stowe had one, as did Colchester, Brattleboro, Cabot, and many other communities. By 1900 there were 186 creameries and 66 cheese factories in the State of Vermont; twenty-four of them were in Chittenden County alone. These creameries were able to establish higher milk quality standards than previously existed. The Creamery in Brattleboro, built in 1887 (village people took most of the stock), raised the price of butter by 12 to 14 cents per pound. They did this by increasing the quality of their butter by continually inspecting the sanitary conditions of farms. Whey from making the cheese was returned to farmers to feed pigs and other livestock.[90, 91]

In the 1890s, the largest butter-making facility was in St. Albans, Vermont, with 60 separators. The Creamery had 1,000 patrons who owned 15,000 cows and in 1892 they made 2,060,000 pounds of butter, the most made any single day being 18,000 pounds. This Creamery had a production capacity of 25,000 pounds per day and still was unable to supply the market's demand for butter.

Butter Production in Vermont

1850. . . .	12 million pounds
1851. . .	15.9 million pounds
1886. . . .	25 million pounds
1899. . . .	35 million pounds
1917. . . .	11 million pounds
1927.	4 million pounds

The quality of Vermont's dairy output was recognized both nationally and internationally. In 1871 over 6,000,000 pounds of butter were exported to Japan alone. This led one observer to suggest that, "By opening the ports of Japan, a market will take all the butter and cheese we have to spare . . . and we need not have any fear of an over supply of delicious butter."[92]

The Board of Agriculture, in its 1893 and 1894 Report, states that, "The quality of Vermont dairy products is pretty well established from competitions made with the world, the two last of which at Paris and Madison Square, both resulted in bringing the gold medal to Vermont, the first instance going to the Moulton Brothers, of Randolph, proprietors of the Green Mountain Stock Farm, and in the latter case to Honorable Homer W. Vail, of Pomfret." The Report further indicates that the advantage to the Vermont farmer is to be within five or six hours of all the principal cities of New England and New York, as it enables the farmer to supply the customer with fresh products when needed.[93]

Butter and Cheese Room

Support Industries to Butter Production

Farmers and creameries took great pride in the packaging and storage of butter for shipment. Butter was commonly packed in wooden tubs with their emblem that distinguished their butter from the butter of other farms. It was estimated in 1870 that the number of tubs needed for Vermont's butter shipments, if set side by side, would reach 230 miles— or, counting 40 tubs to a load, the teams required to draw it would cover 150 miles of road.[94]

According to the catalog of agricultural machines, implements, and tools published in the 1878 Yearbook of Vermont Agriculture, about 575,000 butter tubs were made annually in the State of Vermont, one-half of those in Franklin County. About thirty-four firms made butter tubs, three made butter boxes, and ten made cheese boxes. The firm of

John Hutchins and William Stiles in Montgomery, Vermont, was known for its quality of manufacturing. The firm had four factories employing four hundred men who used 4,000,000 feet of material in a year to make twenty-, thirty-, and fifty-pound tubs. At its peak the company produced 295,000 tubs, many of which were shipped out West.[95]

Another firm that stood out from the many making agricultural implements at the time was the Vermont Farm Machinery Company. Established in the booming river town of Bellows Falls in 1868, it was initially called the Hartford Sorghum Machine Company and made sap evaporators. This equipment was used to boil maple sap in the production of maple syrup, an agricultural endeavor in which Vermont still leads the nation nearly 150 years later.

The firm's name was changed in 1873, and the product line diversified rapidly, evolving toward the dairy industry.[96] The separator, invented by William Cooley of Waterbury in 1877, became their flagship device and was used on most New England farms by the late 1880s.

In addition, Vermont Farm Machinery developed and manufactured a myriad of other lines of equipment, including machine butter churns, presses, bottle washers, coolers, and steam engines and boilers. At one time the largest manufacturer of farm machinery in the world and one of Bellows Falls' most significant employers with hundreds of workers, the company fell on hard times and shuttered the doors of its great three-story brick plant in 1925.[97]

Western Competition

Like most other agricultural industries of the time, Vermont's butter producers faced increasing competition from the West during the late 1800s. In an address to the Vermont Board of Agriculture in 1878, G. S. Fassett of Enosburg illustrated the problem well:

> Consumers of our dairy products said we cannot and will not pay so high for butter and cheese. Western and Southern men saw this to be a golden opportunity for them; they said to themselves, with our shorter winters and immense grain fields, we can make butter for half

of what it costs in the article. They set about it with true grit: and as a result, Illinois, Wisconsin, even Kentucky, and California sent to our markets the real genuine "gilt-edge," driving us out of some of the Western markets and giving us sharp competition in Boston and New York.[98]

In a paper entitled "The Farmer's Future," by Rev. G. F. Wright of Bakersfield, delivered at a meeting of the State Board of Agriculture in St. Albans on March 6 and 7th, 1872, he stated that, "It is useless for the Vermont farmer to compete with those of the West in raising those few staples of product that can be naturally raised in the West, and that will bear storing and transportation without risk of injury, and without too much expense." He went on to say that "the Vermont farmer has a substantial hold on the future. His soil, his climate, his abundance of pure water, and his proximity to markets of the growing cities and villages give him unrivaled facilities for success. Only those who use their minds in studying how to cater to the demands of this growing market and this changing State of things will prosper."[99]

Echoing the sentiments of many others, G. G. Small, Esq. of Morrisville said to the Board that, "Vermont as a State is well adapted to butter making. We cannot compete with the West in beef, pork, wool, or grain, and not much longer in butter unless we are making a superior product."[100]

M. O. Howe of Fayetteville, in the Report of the State Board of Agriculture, 1875–1876, went further, to say that, "It is the value of the products, not the quantity, that indicates the profits of agriculture. There will continue to be the difference of freight and commissions between the markets of the East and the West."[101]

Some seven years later, Lyman W. Peet of Cornwall, Vermont, in a paper presented to the State Board of Agriculture in 1883–84 entitled "Eastern and Western Farming," wrote that, "Only by the use of greater skill and capital by which production shall be cheapened with a quality so superior as to command the highest price in the market, can we hope successfully to meet Western competition."[102]

The Tenth Report of the Board of Agriculture in 1888–1889 noted that, "The selling price of all agricultural commodities tends to approach the lowest cost of production, and the West with cheap feed can produce at less cost than New England."[103]

And soon after, the 15th and 16th Report of the Board of Agriculture for 1894–1895 concluded:

> Our State has seen one industry after another go down under the fierce competition of cheap western land. Our sheep, beef, and grain production have all been borne down through this cause, and today our dairymen are manfully contesting the ground with these same forces.[104]

These individuals, like some before and many after them, were visionaries. They had seen change, had been part of it, and recognized the strengths and competitive advantages of farming in Vermont—that essential benefits were proximity to emerging markets and growing and the high quality of production to meet consumer demands. It was even recognized at this time that "Vermont farmers could not and should not compete with the large 'bonanza farms' of the Western States." It was not practical to do so.[105] Vermont would compete on quality.

Nevertheless, the threat of greater competition from Western producers was always present with the development of rail services connecting the West with the East. An 1879 article in the *Rutland Herald and Globe*, "The Future of The Vermont Farmer," captured the feeling of this period:

> Times are mighty hard, and yet we cannot see any better promise for him in the future; the truth is that the railroads that penetrate the "fresh fields and pastures new" of the West have completely changed the face of our agricultural civilization in New England and the Middle States. In Vermont, dairying is about all that is left to the farmer, and the West will eventually wrest all the profits of that industry from our hands, for every year sees the hold of the East on its old-time employments of agriculture and dairying relaxing, as new railroads are built, and transportation rates are simplified and

reduced by the emulation of the great truck lines; it will not be long before butter and cheese making cease to be profitable.[106]

The Margarine Wars

Another significant economic disruption to the butter market and butter producers was the introduction of oleomargarine, which has an exciting history. It has been written that Napoleon III offered a prize for the formulation of synthetic edible fats as Europe faced a shortage of this nutrition, which he needed for the populace and his army. The prize for this product was awarded in 1869 to French scientist Hippolyte Mège-Mouriès.[107]

A U.S. patent for the production of oleomargarine was granted in 1873 and by 1886 thirty-seven plants were operating in the United States, with many of these in New York State. How much this product might affect the butter trade was unknown, but early concern was genuine. Mark Twain even recorded a conversation overheard between two businessmen aboard the Cincinnati riverboat. In his *Life on the Mississippi*, he wrote, "Why, we are turning out oleomargarine now by thousands of tons. And we can sell it so dirt-cheap that the whole country has got to take it—can't get around it, you see. Butter doesn't stand any show—there ain't any chance for competition."[108]

The reaction to the introduction of oleomargarine from the dairy industry was quick. Organized dairy interests placed articles in publications to incite the public. In a particularly colorful instance, one piece called margarine, "The slag of the butcher shop . . . a compound of diseased hogs and dead dogs."[109] Opposition grew so quickly that in 1882 domestic dairy and butter interests formed the National Association for Prevention of Adulteration of Butter.

State legislatures jumped in to protect butter, too. In 1877, New York and Maryland passed the first labeling laws, and other states soon followed. Laws required the product to be marked, stamped, and branded as such, under a penalty of $100 or imprisonment for thirty days. During 1884 and 1885, state after state banned margarine, its manufacture, and distribution. Vermont was one of five states that attempted to force manufacturers to color any artificial dairy product pink, to make clear that it was not made from real milk or cream.[110]

March 25, 1948

```
Miss Ann Cameron,
141 South Main Street,
White River Junction,Vt.

Dear Miss Cameron:

Your letter of the 19th relative to my vote against the
removal of the oleomargarine tax is received.

 I realize the rapid growth in the use of oleo,and the in-
convenience to the housewife of adding the coloring,but at
the same time I would still object to its being handled in
such a way that the customers of hotels and restaurants
would think they were being served butter.  If some way
could be devised to protect the public from the oleo being
served as butter I would have no objection.

                        Sincerely yours,
```

George Aiken's correspondence gathering support for dairy

The U.S. Supreme Court struck down the state bans, as well as the pink coloration mandate in 1894, finding that under the Interstate Commerce Clause of the U.S. Constitution, "forced adulteration could not be imposed." The Court found that states could, however, *prohibit* coloration, so that margarine producers could not color their product yellow to look more like butter. By 1902, thirty-two states and 80 percent of the U.S. population lived under margarine color bans.

The margarine industry persisted, finding clever ways to work around the ruling. Some of us may remember our mothers talking about the color squeeze mixes added to the uncolored margarine at home. Selling the color as a separate packet was a way for oleo producers to skirt the law that prevented them from selling colored margarine.

Some dairy industry leaders during this time felt that poor-quality butter brought oleomargarine to the market. For example, a former president of the Wisconsin Dairy Association commented in 1880, "Oleomargarine is giving better satisfaction than most dairy butter now made." A speaker from Boston at the annual meeting of the Vermont Dairymen's Association in 1883 stated, "Poor butter is what brought oleomargarine into the market. If we make good butter, we need not be a bit afraid of oleomargarine."[111]

Vermont Congressman Grout: Dairy's Defender

Portrait of William Wallace Grout

Although the margarine bans ultimately failed, Congress had also passed the Federal Margarine Act of 1886, which levied a 2-cent tax on the product and annual registration fees for producers. Vermont Congressman William Wallace Grout had a history of legislative leadership in Vermont, where he had been a member of both the Vermont House and Senate. As Vermont was a predominant dairy state and was called the Butter Capital of the World, it was not surprising that he introduced a significant piece of legislation to the U.S. House that amended the 1886 Margarine Act in favor of the dairy industry. The debate was highly charged: those arguing for margarine argued that it served the needs of the economically needy.[112] Congressman Grout, supported by a well-organized dairy and butter lobby, made the following case:

- Margarine was a deceptive work of man, a counterfeit item.

- The product would have a ruinous effect, as it was dishonest competition on the most significant agricultural industry in the United States.

- The purpose of the legislation was not to raise revenue for the country but to regulate the sale of an article of commerce.

When Justin Morrill died on December 28, 1898, after thirty-one years representing Vermont in the U.S. Senate, the competition for his seat pitted Governor William Dillingham against Congressman Grout, both Republicans. It was reported at the time that, "As the race got nastier, both candidates started slinging mud—or, more accurately, butter." According to the history of the times, since Grout had a strong record of championing dairy farmers in Washington, Governor Dillingham tried to portray himself as equally supportive. "Grout made the

Portrait of William Paul Dillingham

startling charge that Dillingham . . . [was] a paid operator for the political margarine machine." Dillingham fired back, defending his record as a butter protector. He said he supported a law to prevent the sale of colored margarine and, if elected, would support Grout's bill to tax margarine and ban colored margarine nationwide." Ultimately, Dillingham, elected to the U.S. Senate, would serve until 1923. Grout retired to his farm in 1901 and died soon after.[113]

Grout's amendment to the Margarine Act would not be passed into law until 1902, but it still bore his name. The Grout Bill imposed a 10 cents per pound tax on all colored margarine and ¼ cents per pound on uncolored margarine. This tax system, together with the outright bans on colored margarine in some states, firmly established the margarine-industry practice of selling an uncolored product with color squeeze packets that consumers could add at home, like many of our mothers did, to make the margarine look more like butter.

Vermont butter production, which had peaked in 1899 at 35 million pounds, plummeted in the early years of the 20th century, to 11 million pounds by 1917 and to just 4 million pounds ten years later. Attempts to prohibit or reduce margarine production and distribution through various means—including color, fines, and taxation—could not overcome consumer interest in lower-cost products. When imitation products began to be manufactured with oils from corn, soy, and other vegetable products, the dairy industry was pitted against other agricultural interests, not just the livestock fats and the Chicago slaughterhouses. Margarine consumption increased during the Depression and World War II eras, and overtook butter consumption in 1957.[114]

(For readers who would enjoy a light-hearted survey of the butter-margarine wars, a contemporary film called *Margarine Wars* depicts this period as a comedy. It shows with humor the story of the son of a Swedish dairy farmer in Wisconsin duped into smuggling margarine into his state.)[115]

Today, the pendulum has swung back the other way: the average American consumes 16 pounds of butter and only 2.8 pounds of margarine per year.[116] Today's dairy industry, however, faces competition from a new wave of products: imitation "milks" made from crops like oats and almonds.

CHAPTER FIVE

Agricultural Research and Education

ERMONT FARMERS had seen one agricultural crop after another come under severe Western competition in the 1800s as increased settlement there took place and increased transportation became available. It happened first with grain in the Champlain Valley, and then with Merino sheep, and with butter too.

The land available to farmers and ranchers as the West was developed was immense. Major changes in federal laws in the 1860s opened the West to greater settlement and, with the railroads, resulted in increased agricultural competition with markets in the East: "With the Homestead Act of 1862, in just a few decades, an enormous amount of land, roughly equal to all Western Europe, was made available to ranchers and farmers."[117.] This change in available land and its use for agricultural production would have a profound and lasting impact on farm production and product competition in markets in the East.

A report on the antitrust status of early farmer cooperatives documents that, "The increase of agricultural production was closely related to the increase in population. Cheap railroad rates enabled the more remote farmers to compete with farmers raising farm produce on the seacoast, and their dressed meat and grain were sent to consumers thousands of miles away."[118.] The Report goes on to say that, "In 1869, the Golden Spike ceremony commemorating the joining of the Union

Pacific with the Central Pacific marked the advent of transatlantic rail service."[119] California agricultural products could now be shipped to the East in a matter of days instead of weeks.

Emigration from Vermont had reached 200,000, according to the 1870 census.[120] By the 1870s, farms in the state continued to be abandoned, especially on the less agriculturally productive hillsides and more marginal lands. Young people and families were moving elsewhere, especially after the Civil War, in search of better opportunities. By 1895, the Vermont Board of Agriculture was advertising over one hundred and twenty-five farms for sale in the state.[121] This immigration hollowed out many rural communities in the state.

Education for Farmers

College education in 1850 was for white men with money, and most studied theology, medicine, or law. At this time, 80 percent of Americans lived in rural areas, and 60 percent of these were farmers.

The second half of the century brought increased attention to education and organization to advance farming as it became more mechanized and industrialized. It was recognized by many that the West, with its vast land resources and railroads, would become an increasingly competitive threat to agriculture in Vermont and the region. Better education was one solution, and Vermont was an early leader in this effort.

Vermont's 1777 Constitution is said to be the first in English-speaking North America to mandate public funding for universal education and to provide public education for girls. Education is the only government service that has ever been accorded constitutional status in the state. One contemporary observer has commented that, "Education is as much a Vermont tradition as maple syrup, winter sports, and the Green Mountains." It was the first state to constitutionally guarantee an articulated education system, beginning with primary schools and concluding with a university.[122]

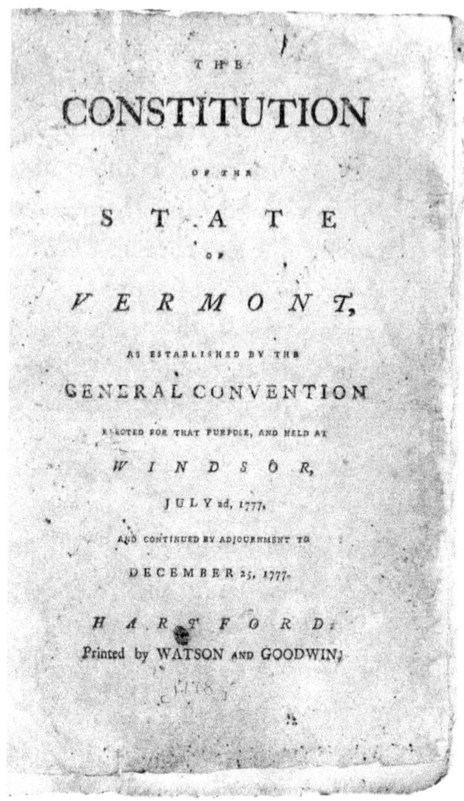

The Constitution of the State of Vermont

Influence of European Models on Agricultural Education

Several agricultural societies and schools in 18th-century Europe taught and practiced agriculture. These approaches became of interest in the New World. For example, Ben Franklin established the American Philosophical Society in 1743 and was an early member of the Pennsylvania Society for Promoting Agriculture, founded in 1785. These early societies were formed around the landed gentry at the time and did not address the interest of the common folks. The Berkshire Agricultural Society in Massachusetts, formed in 1811, was considered one of the first to do so. The founder of that society, Elkanah Watson, advocated the involvement of the community in the first full-blown local fair that was organized from the bottom up. He subscribed to the Jeffersonian idea that farmers were the backbone of society. This approach to the involvement of the community in these local events was the beginning of the "Golden Age of agricultural education and knowledge between 1850 and 1870."[123]

By the 1840s and 1850s, county agricultural societies had been formed in Vermont and many other parts of New England. A principal purpose of the organization was holding an annual exhibit, or fair. Farm families brought their best livestock, produce, baked goods, and needlework, competing for blue ribbons. They exchanged information about improving the quality of their crops, and they enjoyed the opportunities for social exchange and good fun. By 1860, 941 of these societies had been formed in the United States and had begun to exert a powerful influence on agricultural policies and agricultural education within the United States.[124]

Calvacade state fair, 1909

In Vermont, the Caledonia Cattle Fair was organized as early as 1834. After 1838, annual shows were held for several years, eventually superseded by the Caledonia County Agricultural Society, founded in 1844 in St. Johnsbury. The Society's first county fair was held that year. Soon after, the Rutland County Agricultural Society was formed and held its first fair in 1846 at Castleton. Except for 1917, when no fair was held in the state because of a polio epidemic, the Rutland fair has been an annual event ever since. In the 1840s, yearly fairs began in Bennington, St. Albans, Burlington, Orleans County, and Addison County. In September 1853, a Vermont State Fair was held on Seminary Hill (later the site of Vermont College) in Montpelier. Prizes at these fairs were generally provided with the aid of state appropriations and fairground ticket proceeds.[125] Other fairs began later, including the Tunbridge World's Fair in 1867.

Attendance today at any of Vermont's county fairs brings back the history of the county fair concept and the folksy charm of its attractions. Besides the cattle and animal shows, there are events for youth and displays on locally produced products and awards, as well as the history of the fair itself. They showcase the importance of getting the community together to advance the knowledge of and interest in agriculture and local food systems.[126]

The Vermont State Agricultural Society

It was almost inevitable that Fredrick Holbrook would be the founder and first president of the Vermont State Agricultural Society in 1850. He was passionate about agriculture and farming and lived at that time in a part of Vermont (Windham County) where agriculture was important. The Windham County Agricultural Society had been established in 1843.

Raised in Brattleboro, Holbrook made an extended trip to Europe in his youth to learn how they practiced agriculture. Holbrook took advantage of the farming knowledge gained in Europe, becoming a farmer and writer advocating for improved methods. He experimented and invented on his farm, and among the implements he designed was the all-steel plow. In the 1850s, Holbrook became an associate editor of the *New England Farmer* magazine and president of the Vermont State Agricultural Society, serving eight years as the leader. Various societies had been created on the county level by the 1850s, and it was only logical that a state organization be established.[127]

The state agricultural societies were a powerful national advocacy body when they created the United States Agricultural Society in 1852, which influenced the enactment of the Land Grant College Act and the establishment of the U.S. Department of Agriculture in 1862.[128] State ag societies were also influential in establishing boards of agriculture in many states. Vermont created its Board of Agriculture in 1870, following the example of New York in 1819, New Hampshire in 1820, and Massachusetts in 1852.

Holbrook was active during this formative period. Elected governor of Vermont in 1861, he retired soon after in 1862. When Cornell College of Agriculture was established in 1868, Holbrook was appointed a nonresident professor of mechanics applied to agriculture[129] and was required to provide twenty lectures per academic year. Appointed the first board member of the State Board of Agriculture, Manufacturing, and Mining in 1870, he resigned shortly after, but resumed his farm and business interests including as an associate editor of the *New England Farmer* magazine. While he did not run again for elected office, his interest in agriculture continued both on his farm, as an inventor, and as a writer of information on agriculture and farming. He returned to farming and as a writer addressing agricultural issues of importance.

From Agricultural Societies to Land Grant Colleges

While agricultural societies helped bring information to local farmers and their families, the need for better forms of higher education was also recognized and advocated. This was not a new idea; it was something that agricultural societies were in favor of. As early as 1787, George Washington proposed a national public university for agriculture and the sciences.[130] (Washington once declared, "I'd rather be on my farm than be emperor of the world.") Several private colleges and universities, such as Yale, Harvard, and Amherst, had agricultural science courses. In 1838 there was a proposal to use a grant from James Smithson (founder of the Smithsonian Institution) to establish a national agricultural college.[131] In 1850, Illinois College Professor Jonathan Baldwin Turner proposed providing liberal education to farmers, factory workers, and others through public land appropriation.[132] The Illinois legislature sent the idea to Congress in 1853. Captain Alden Partridge, the founder of Norwich University and a former Commandant of West Point, had proposed a national system of higher education covering courses in farming, engineering, and business financed by the sale of public lands.[133] He also was a friend of Justin Morrill, who was the Senator who wrote and had President Lincoln sign the Land Grant Act in 1862.

Land Grant Act

Portrait of Justin Smith Morrill

Justin Smith Morrill entered Congress in 1855,[134] several years after Jonathan Turner and others had already proposed many ideas for a national public education system for agriculture.[135] A friend of Captain Partridge's, Morrill understood the importance of education from his own background. Building on this knowledge, he first proposed the establishment of one or more schools of agriculture based on the military academy concept.[136] Further work was needed, and he relied on others for guidance. These included Turner of Illinois, New York farmer Ezra Cornell, and newspaper publisher Horace Greeley. After a five-year struggle, the first Land Grant Bill passed the House by the slimmest of margins. President Buchanan vetoed it, saying the country was too poor and the law was unconstitutional. The bill was reintroduced in 1861 in the new Congress at a time of great strife in the country. Supporters promoted the law as a way to repair the ravages of the Civil War and safeguard the country by offering new educational opportunities to a fragile and divided country at the time of the Land Grant Act. By the time of Lincoln signing the law several members of the Southern congressional delegation had departed the Union. The Land Grant bill passed both houses of Congress by wide margins, without the Southern delegation, and was signed into law by President Lincoln in 1862.[137]

Morrill's Land Grant Act of 1862 was the first time a nation created a public higher education system. The act was considered a historic achievement that changed the course of agriculture in the United States:

> Andrew White, for many years the President of Cornell University and later Minister to Germany, rated Senator Justin Morrill's work very high. He stated that it was his opinion that the Land Grant Act deserves to be ranked with those of Hamilton in advocating the U.S. Constitution, Jefferson in acquiring Louisiana, and Clay in giving us a truly American Policy.[138]

Two months before signing the Land Grant Act, President Lincoln had approved the Homestead Act, opening up "public land"—what had been Native American lands—to settlers and resulting in the eventual appropriation of 120 million acres during the duration of the law.[139] At the same time, with the Pacific Railway Act, Lincoln had granted the railroads more than 175 million acres of Native American land, an area more than one-tenth of the whole United States.[140] These laws helped assure the West's rapid development.[141] With the vast amount of land available, it was not too much to ask, then, for a mere 17 million acres to be granted to the states (based on 30,000 acres to each member of Congress from each state), the proceeds of which would go to establish Land Grant Colleges in each state. Eastern states that did not have public land received scripts they could assign.[142]

Organizing the Vermont Land Grant College

Vermont was one of the first three states to accept the land grant. The Vermont legislature passed a law in 1863 providing a provision for one Land Grant Institution by joining the University of Vermont with Middlebury College and Norwich University. Several others strongly supported this joint structure. It did not happen, as the trustees of the various institutions that needed to embrace the concept did not endorse it. When it did not occur, Senator Morrill offered a $5,000 challenge grant if built in the town of Strafford. When that effort failed as well, the then-private University of Vermont offered to become the Land Grant institution of the state.[143]

In a testament to foresight, the Land Grant concept was not established solely for the purpose of teaching agriculture. The Act intended to allow those engaged in industrial pursuits to acquire further knowledge of the practical sciences related to agriculture and the mechanical arts.

The University of Vermont as a Land Grant College

The University of Vermont became one of the first three Land Grant Colleges in the United States. Still, it was an alliance not fully supported by the Vermont farm community, which was not uncommon for the time. Dartmouth College became a Land Grant, as did others like Brown University in Rhode Island and Yale University, but they did not remain so.[144] The relationship between a private institution of higher learning and a farm community is one of trust-building through relationships and these privately established institutions did not have the deep and lasting connections with the farm community needed to establish trust. It was therefore not surprising that in 1890 the Vermont State Grange, a politically powerful organization at the time, argued that the College of Agriculture could not do its best work when connected to the University of Vermont.[145]

The Grange Movement

The Grange movement, or what was known as the Patrons of Husbandry, was founded in Washington, D.C. in 1867 at a time when technological developments, including railroads, were threatening rural lifestyles. The organization quickly galvanized community support through inclusive membership, including the placement of women in active roles. Its objective was to bring as many members from the community into membership to address farm and community needs, and it quickly became a political force in local communities. Vermont became the first state in New England and only the seventh state in the U.S. to form a Grange in 1872. Unlike the local agricultural societies that addressed local fairs for educational and community involvement, the Grange became an activist organization at the local, state, and national levels. It promoted the strengthening of rural America through grassroots activities.[146]

In Vermont in 1890, the Grange demanded that the state legislature dissolve the partnership between the University of Vermont and the College of Agriculture, saying that Land Grant funds had been used for purposes other than agricultural education.[147] UVM, it argued, still needed to grant a single diploma to an agricultural student in the twenty-five years since the University became a Land Grant institution.

A bill was introduced in the Vermont legislature to create the Vermont State Agricultural and Mechanical College, separate from the University of Vermont. Hearings in the Vermont Legislature were held on the proposal put forth by the Grange. Justin Morrill, however, testified in support of UVM as the Land Grant Institution, and the push to create a new and separate Land Grant College failed in the Vermont Senate. Senator Morrill had been the supporter of UVM, Middlebury, and Norwich being one Land Grant in the beginning and clearly felt in being asked to testify that the University of Vermont should retain the Land Grant that any change to create a new Land Grant in Vermont would be too disruptive. The College of Agriculture would remain at the University of Vermont thereafter.

Breaking ground for the new Grange Hall, Williamsville, Vermont

Nevertheless, it remained a questionable alliance with the Vermont farm community, and eventually, in 1912, the state would create the Carnegie Foundation Survey, a commission to investigate the educational system and conditions in Vermont. Its report stated that "The situation in which the College of Agriculture finds itself, the lack of equipment, the empirical quality of its courses, and the failure to connect with industries of the State, is the result of a policy of the Administration for which the trustees are responsible." In conclusion, the Foundation found that, "It is our fifty years of experience in agricultural education that a trade school will not grow in a University atmosphere."[148]

These challenges were not unique to the Land Grant concept in Vermont. In New Hampshire, the distant relationship between Dartmouth and the farm community resulted in the creation of the University of New Hampshire. Similarly in Rhode Island, Brown University had been the designated Land Grant institution before the formation of the University of Rhode Island. Likewise Yale University, which remained a Land Grant College for 60 years, gave up its status to Storrs or the University of Connecticut in 1893. In each case, the farm community and the Grange were instrumental in bringing about the changes that arose from concerns that local agricultural education needs were not being adequately addressed.

The Vermont State Agricultural Experiment Station

Unlike its counterparts elsewhere in New England, UVM ultimately retained its Land Grant College status, though it would be decades before it built a true alliance with the farming community. Meanwhile, with the support of the Vermont State Board of Agriculture and the Federal Hatch Act of 1887 that authorized the creation of State Agricultural Experiment Stations, Vermont created the Vermont State Agricultural Experiment Station and placed it under the charge of the University of Vermont and State Agricultural College. According to the announcement of the Station by the Board of Control, it was compelled by, "The wish to make the Station as widely useful as its resources will admit. Every Vermont citizen concerned with agriculture, whether farmer, manufacturer, or dealer, has the right to apply to the Station for any assistance rendered within its province. The Station will respond to all applications as far as its power."[149] The first annual report indicated that a farm had been purchased with suitable buildings erected and stocked so that the Vermont Station at the time would be able to carry out work in the following areas:

- Farm crop experimentation, stock feeding, fruit and vegetable adaptation to the soil and climate of the state

- Plant diseases

- Impact of insects on vegetation

- Fertilizer analysis

- Miscellaneous chemical work which farmers of the state sent in

At the time, the Hatch Act required that bulletins or progress reports be published at each station at least once in three months; these reports were to be sent to the newspapers in the state where the station was located.

The New Dean at the College of Agriculture in the Early 1900s Brought a Greater Focus to UVM's Land Grant Role

Basement dairy operation in Morrill Hall, University of Vermont

The road to a real partnership between farmers and university was long and slow. According to former University of Vermont Dean Robert Sinclair, "Decades of effort, distinguished by the leadership of Dean Joseph Hills and Dean Joseph Carrigan, were still required to bridge the gap between rural Vermonters, suspicious of book farming, and the University of Vermont's tradition of classical learning." By 1900, when Hills received the title of Dean, thirty-five years after the formation of UVM and the State Agriculture College, the state at last had a School of Agriculture, both in substance and in name. Still, it had taken a major threat from the legislature to separate the College from the University before UVM was willing to honor its commitment.[150] It was the threat to take away the Land Grant designation away from the University of Vermont that led Dean Hills to move to build support within the farm community in the state.

Dean Hills, according to Sinclair, recognized the importance of the College of Agriculture's connection to rural Vermont and the farm community. Before the arrival of federal funding for county extension work (Smith-Lever Act of 1914), Hills received state support to fund three agents to conduct relationship work. The Extension Service, as it became known, and its connection with the Experiment Station and University became the critical link to the farming community. It was a link the College of Agriculture badly needed: a partnership and direct connection with farmers. The county extension system was instrumental in the creation of the three-legged stool of of Research, Teaching, and Extension Education.[151]

Technical Education: Creation of the State School of Agriculture in Randolph

T. G. Bronson of Hardwick, a noted Jersey breeder and then Chair of the Vermont House Agriculture Committee, was the father of a bill creating the State School of Agriculture in Randolph in 1910. The Vermont Dairymen's Association had called for the state's support of a secondary school of agriculture in 1908, and the state Grange had pushed for it as well.

A Vermont school superintendent of the time would often say, before the creation of the State School of Agriculture, that "If a Vermont lad wished to secure training in agriculture within state borders and was not fit to enter the College of Agriculture, he needed to commit a crime."[152] He would then enter the Reform School in Vergennes, the only place in Vermont where agriculture was taught at the secondary school level. The need for education of youth instead of receiving a four-year college degree was well recognized at this time, where students could receive hands-on applied education on all aspects of farming. This called for a secondary school of agriculture and thus the designation of the Randolph Normal School by the Vermont legislature as the location for the Vermont School of Agriculture in 1910.

CHAPTER SIX

Rural Life in Crisis

THE 1890 U.S. CENSUS DECLARED THE WEST SETTLED, and across the country a trend toward urbanization was well underway.[153] Though a majority of Americans still lived in rural communities and on farms, the number was decreasing rapidly as America transformed from a rural agrarian society into an urban industrial one. Vermont was experiencing the impact of this change: "84.8 percent of the population was rural in 1890 versus 67 percent in 1930. Also, in 1850 more than 60 percent of the Vermont towns contained more than 1,000 people; in 1930, fewer than 40 percent of them were of that size."[154, 155] The abandonment of many hilltop farms became an issue during this time. The State Board of Agriculture issued a catalog describing 200 Vermont farms without tenants and on the market for a meager price.[156]

The state legislature in 1888 established a new position, Commissioner of Agriculture and Manufacturing, in response to widespread concern among state leaders about the decline of rural Vermont, both in population numbers and in the quality of life of its inhabitants and the focus on non-native-born Vermonters versus others. Since before the Civil War, many Vermonters were leaving the state, and this was noticeable with the loss of hilltop farms. Many communities in rural areas were being disrupted and new attempts were being made to address this problem.

During this time, the state reached out to Sweden to bring people to take over some hilltop farms.[157] Rooted in prejudice and fear, the effort was at least in part a response to the arrival of French Canadians who took up tenancy at some of Vermont's abandoned hilltop farms. One historical society article put a fine point on the common sentiment of the time:

> Valentine, the appointed Commissioner, focused on Scandinavians because he considered them superior to the undesirable people of French-Canadian heritage who at the time were often settling on these farms.[158]

By 1890 about one-third of Vermont's residents were first- or second-generation French Canadians. To find an acceptable alternative to an increase in the population of French Canadians, Valentine looked at the Swedes in Maine occupying public land and the Union Pacific railroad colonies in the West. He even employed John G. Edgen, a Swede from Nebraska, and sent him to Sweden to find good farmers and citizens. Members of the 27 families selected landed in New York in 1890. These immigrants were in three colonies in Vermont: Wilmington in Windham County, Weston in Windsor County, and Vershire in Orange County.

While they became good citizens, the colonies did not work out as planned. The Swedes moved on, never establishing the cohesive colonies that Valentine hoped would attract more. Eventually the program was terminated by the legislature. Victor Spear of the State Board of Agriculture summarized the effort, conceding that, "It wasn't work adapted to Vermont, and the theory was wrong."[159]

The Searls article suggests that historians are interested in the story of "Valentine's Swedes" for several reasons.[160] The report illustrates the degree to which the state's Gilded Age elite saw its farming districts as being in a crisis. Controversy over the program is also evidence of the deep divisions between urban and rural perspectives that characterized Vermont society, manifesting in state politics and culture. It suggests the extent to which state leaders did not perceive that the purchase of farmsteads as summer homes rather than as working farms would be, to a large extent, the future of rural Vermont. It speaks volumes to how the state's urban-minded leaders profoundly misunderstood the sources and character of the solid communal bonds that knit together the dwellers of small towns. Perhaps most of all, the story illustrates the pervasive anti-

Catholic bias of the era, mainly as it applied to immigrants from Quebec and their descendants.

After this so-called fiasco, the state legislature doubled its support to the State Board of Agriculture while requiring the Board to make a "complete report as to unoccupied farms." According to a *Rutland Herald* article, the result was less a comprehensive set of proposed action and more of, "A List of Desirable Farms at Low Prices." The article went on to say:

> The facts for Vermont appear to be as follows: The State is in a condition of rapid, almost violent, industrial and social change. There are now six times as many towns in Vermont, having a population of 2,000 or more than in 1850. The urban and suburban population is growing more rapidly than the rural population is decreasing. While rural towns are becoming suburban and urban, and many of the hill towns are becoming depleted of population and are growing into forests, in the intermediate class of towns, farming is becoming so much more scientific and intensive that the total of farm products is never greater than now, and there is constant increase. People are just beginning to know how to adjust themselves to the natural resources and to the new industrial civilization which begins to pulsate in the Green Mountain valleys as in the rest of the world. New railroads and trolley lines, rural telephones and free mail routes, the co-operative creamery, the town system of schools providing numerous excellent town high schools, the Grange and other farmers' organizations, thriving summer hotels, improved farm machinery, better-constructed highways, and various other agencies are making of Vermont a new state.[161]

Sentiment for the Land

From all indications, there was a sizable sentiment for the land during the late nineteenth century—for the pastoral landscape and wilderness. It emerged at a time when the northern New England hill country was experiencing economic readjustment. According to the State Board of Agriculture in 1895, Vermonters were learning that scenery has economic value. The Central Vermont Railroad remarked in the same year that, "The area of tilled land is growing less in Vermont . . . agriculture is retreating to the more easily tilled soil of the valleys and abandoning the farms on the hills," while in the same breath, urged those seeking rest and change to buy unoccupied property as summer homes.

What began as a crusade to repopulate rural districts with farmers bloomed into a full-scale effort to attract a broader market. That market was more responsive every year. In 1906, the Vergennes *Enterprise and Vermonter* announced that the summer business of the 1905 season had been the largest in the state's history in similar activities. Vermont had gone virtually unnoticed during previous decades, while the rest of northern New England and New York State had seen tremendous growth as resort areas. Notably, Vermont led the others in the systematic advancement of summer attractions by the state; in 1911, the legislature took over the job of promotion from the railroads and the Board of Agriculture, establishing a Board of Publicity as part of the Department of State.[162]

In her book, *The Selling of Vermont*, the author Andrea Rebek states that "At some future day, the landscape of Vermont—our hills and Valleys, our waterfalls and brooklets—will be considered second to none in beauty and grandeur."[163] In the decades that followed, tourism would become an essential part of Vermont's attractions and a growing sector of the state's economy. Vermont was becoming a favorite resort destination for those who wanted to escape the city, and many sought homes on the farms. In the 1904 Report of the State Board of Agriculture, the Board's Secretary C. J. Bell states that "The pamphlet published last year by the Board, advertising the resources and attractions of Vermont, has had excellent circulation. The Board distributed several thousand to every State in the Union and many to foreign countries. This significant effort resulted in the sale of many of these unoccupied farms and enticing city boarders to hotels in the state."[164]

The Country Life Commission

Concerns about the shifting land use and the culture changes that came with it had many observers concerned. Progressives in the early 1900s felt that, "Even rural neighborhoods in the twentieth century had lost the sense of community characteristic of the nineteenth century." Some believed that the same decadence of city life that led to the fall of Rome was working its way into Vermont. They saw the decline of the rural population ultimately affecting the nation's welfare.

President Teddy Roosevelt appointed a Country Life Commission in 1908 to address these concerns.[165, 166] The Commission had three objectives for the improvement of rural life:

- A national agricultural extension program

- Scientific surveys of rural life

- The establishment of a federal agency devoted to rural progress

In the 1909 First Annual Report of the Commissioner of Agriculture, an essay by E. S. Brigham, entitled "The Outlook for Vermont Farming," cited an article in *The World's Work* by a member of President Roosevelt's Country Life Commission.[167] It stated, "After some months of investigation, the country sees communication; education adapted to the development of the land and the people, and then it needs organization." Brigham went on to say that "the well-being of Vermont agriculture is to be determined by our utilization of these three great agencies of progress: organization, communication, and education."

He further elaborated in an article on hillside farms, writing that, "The production of crops on these hillside farms, at a profit large enough to enable a man to live today as the world lives, is impossible in competition with the more easily machine-tilled field. The level lands of the Champlain Valley and the hillsides of the lower altitudes offer opportunities in the production of fruit at a larger income per acre than is now being derived from the present cropping system." Nevertheless

"*Greetings from Vermont*" postcard, 1939

"*Come to the Green Mountains of Vermont*" pamphlet

"Canadian Gateway" tourist map

Mt. Mansfield Smugglers' Notch, Vt. postcard

he concludes this article on a note of optimism, stating that, "I believe that under the leadership of the agricultural college, the Commissioner of agriculture, and the agricultural press, we are entering upon an era of better things when there will be a better organization of our farms, more cooperation, and united effort, a more perfect means of communication, and a broader education for all. Believing these things, I feel that the outlook for Vermont farming is very hopeful."

Others expressed similar needs. The President of the Vermont Dairymen's Association, in his address in 1908 noted that, "Cooperation should be our watch-word and guide. What we mean by this is meeting, talking, working, buying and selling, and acting together for our mutual interest."[168]

The Country Church

Many in the Country Life Movement in the United States in the early 1900s identified the country church as a critical institution in the reform of rural life. The country church had declined and needed to be revitalized, according to the Country Life Commission and its members. Undertaking studies of how these churches could best be restored came through work conducted by Charles Otis Gill, a graduate of Yale and Yale Divinity School and Union Theological Seminary. His early work in Vermont was as a Congregational minister in Hartland. Gill, along with Gifford Pinchot, also a Yale graduate and a member of the Country Life

Portrait of Gifford Pinchot

Commission, authored two influential books on the state of rural churches in America with remedies for the revitalization of rural life. Pinchot, already distinguished as a leading conservationist, would go on to serve as the first head of the U.S. Forest Service.

Their first book, *The Country Church*, published in 1913, studied rural churches in two counties: one in Windsor County in Vermont and the other in Tompkins County, New York, the home of Cornell University and the home of Liberty Hyde Bailey, who had been Chair of the Country Life Commission.[169] The purpose of these studies and resulting books was, "To help in getting the country church back into the position it ought to occupy as a great power working effectively for country life."

Gill and Pinchot, as well as others in the Country Life Movement, had identified the country church as a critical institution in the reform of rural life. The church, they recognized, had declined but needed to be revived or restored to its "old time" vitality by a new program of social service. Thus, the country church was seen as a force for community improvement. Pinchot, as a member of the Country Life Commission, believed, as did Gill, that the country church could take a role in making rural life a success by organizing cooperative ventures in crop production, marketing, milling, banking, and purchasing of supplies. The church needed to reestablish itself as a leader in the community and farm life as it had been in the nineteenth century.

It was no surprise then that Vermont Governor Fairbanks chose Charles Otis Gill as a delegate to the North American Commission.[170] This Commission, created by President Wilson in 1913, was established to address further rural and farmer concerns raised by the Country Life Commission and others at the time. It consisted of representatives from many of the states plus four Canadian provinces and was challenged and authorized to "investigate, and study in European Countries cooperatives, land-mortgage banks, cooperative rural credit unions, and similar organizations and institutions, devoting their attention to the promotion of agriculture and the betterment of rural conditions." One commentary of the time stated:

> The great American Commission sent to Europe in 1913, composed of many of America's ablest agricultural leaders, brought home from there a vast amount of information that was of great value in promoting renewed cooperative effort in America in the recent period of most significant economic development.[171]

They undertook this mission in travels and meetings throughout Europe, Russia, and Egypt in three months, from April to July 1913. This comprehensive study and journey, and the resulting report helped to usher in fundamental and lasting institutional changes in the United States. Among the most impactful outcomes came when Congress created the federally authorized Agricultural Extension Service in 1914 and established the Federal Farm Credit Land Banks two years later.

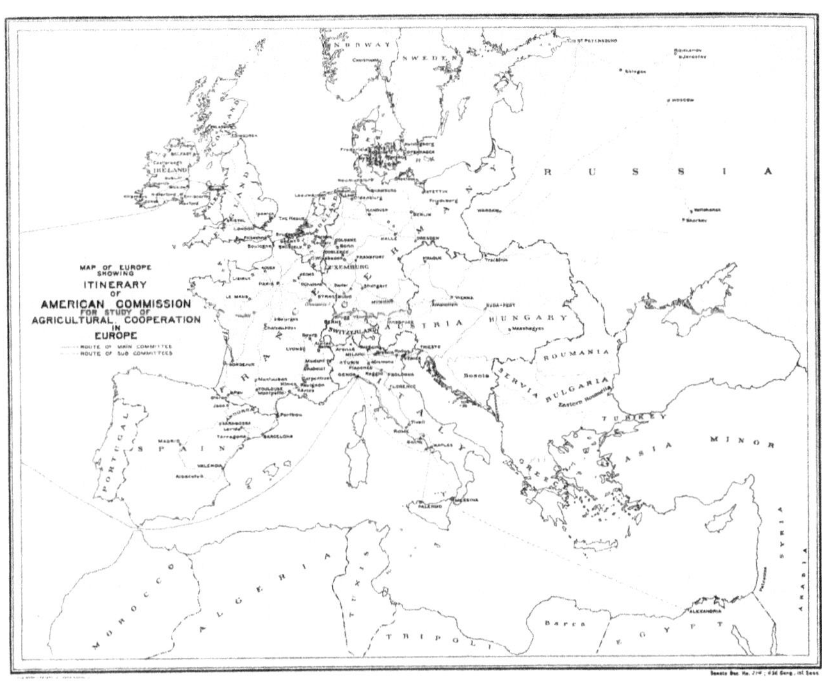

Charles Otis Gill's European Commission Map

After his return as a member of the Commission and a review of the conditions in Europe, Gill joined Pinchot to continue their investigation of country churches and follow-up their study of the two counties in Vermont and New York. The conclusion of their previous study led to the creation of the Commission on Church and Country Life and it was decided to extend the analysis to an entire state, for which Ohio was chosen. The study, *Six Thousand Country Churches*, by Gill and Pinchot, was published in 1919 and was considered one of the most thorough studies of country churches and their role in rural America at the time.[172] In their findings, the authors wrote that, "Unless a larger and stronger social and religious institution is created in the country districts than is now found in the country church, the more vigorous young people will, for the most part, leave the country. . . ."[173]

Other Interesting Happenings
in Vermont Agriculture During This Time

- The Vermont General Assembly passed the Creamery Inspection Act in 1912, which required the inspection twice each year of plants where dairy products are handled.

- The need for product diversity on the farm was recognized. In the *Thirty-Fourth Annual Report of the Vermont Dairymen's Association in 1904* (page 32), a farmer stated " . . . but when we consider the gradual widening out of the dairy production (westward), the high price of labor, mishaps that follow along with a herd of cows, the ups and downs of the seasons in their influence upon the fodder supply, all having a tendency to narrow in the profits it is well, I think, for Vermont dairymen to stop and consider if there is not an opportunity for them to make a combination of dairying with one or more sidelines, thereby making farming more profitable to them and more sought after by their family.

- The Honorable Joseph A. DeBoer, President of National Life Insurance Co., stated in an article submitted to *New England Farmer* in 1905 and reprinted in the *Brattleboro Reformer* in 1905, that due to increased distribution of products from the West, to a large extent the advantage is against local farms. He said emphatically that local markets are the best for the farmer, and they are the point of special interest. It is necessary to study what they need, and what the markets will pay the most for, and these markets can be kept and maintained. He went on to say that the nearest market is the best, the most reliable, and costs less to reach.

- The number of cow testing associations increased from 36 to 42 in 1916.

- In 1904, according to the Agricultural Report of the State Board of Agriculture, seven canning factories were operating in Vermont (Westminster, Northfield, Windsor, Brattleboro, Waterbury, St. Albans, and Essex Junction). Sweet corn represented 98 percent of the operations.

- In 1907 it was stated in the Vermont Agriculture Report of the State Board of Agriculture that it was hoped that when Morrill Hall opened at UVM that there would be a course on cheese making as there was a need for more excellent uniformity in quality.

- In 1910 and 1911, the Rutland Railroad and the Central Vermont Railroad placed a "Better Farming Special" train with cars at the disposal of the State Department of Agriculture and the State College of Agriculture for the instruction of farming communities in the state. It was discontinued in 1912 as Boston and Maine would not participate.

- During the First World War, a Farmers' War Council was organized. The State Department of Agriculture and the Extension Service cooperated to aid in increasing food production in the state. James Hartness of Springfield was appointed State Food Commissioner. He was assisted by John Cushing, editor of the *St. Albans Messenger* (Vol. 4, *History of Vermont*).

CHAPTER SEVEN

Cooperation and Regulation

I N THE EARLY 1900S, Vermont dairy farming was moving to fluid milk production to supply the cities, and away from the butter and cheese production for which the state had long been known. Before milk became an export, farmers sent their cream to local creameries where butter and cheese were produced.[174] Moving away from this type of localized, value-added production to fluid milk production on the farm was a significant change. By 1922, 50 percent of the milk and 62 percent of the New England cream received in the Boston market came from Vermont.[175] Vermont had the highest dairy production per capita of any state and its economy was the most dependent on the dairy sector. Also, since the demise of the Merino sheep industry in the 1850s, dairy production had migrated to the better river valley lands within the state, which led to the continued loss of hilltop farms as people moved to the urban areas or moved out of state. Sending milk from farms to the cities created new challenges, including fair buyer pricing, railroad shipping rates, and sanitary regulations with interstate shipments. It would also result in the closure of many of the local creameries operating in towns throughout the state.[176]

In the face of increasing competition from the West, Vermont recognized that the advantages its farming sector possessed were being near the markets and having valued, high quality products backed by production standards and grades. Adjustment of these strengths to the needs of distant buyers would require time and cooperation among farmers.

Bottling milk, 1917

The Grange in the late 1800s nationally and within Vermont became an organization seeking value for farmers and the communities that they were part of: "The Grange laws were a turning point because they reversed a longstanding trend of decreasing government regulation of the private sector."[177] In Vermont the Grange became a voice for reform, seeking a reduction in railroad rates for farmers, and for the growth of cooperatives.

Nationally, the Sherman Antitrust Act took on the breakup of Standard Oil and other monopolies in 1890. While the railroads had provided transportation and business access across the land, they also became the first businesses to be subject to anticompetitive conduct.[178]

At the time the Sherman Act was being considered by Congress, there were about 1,000 active farmer cooperatives in the U.S.: more than 700 dairy cooperatives, about 100 grain cooperatives, and about 100 fruit and vegetable cooperatives.[179] Many of the leaders of the time saw education, organization, and cooperation in marketing as being critical and essential for the future and for being able to compete with the West for markets. "Co-operation all along . . . should be the watchword and bent and trend of the teachings in every agricultural meeting throughout our land," stated the President of the Vermont Dairymen's Association in 1907."[180]

Vermont's Commissioner of Agriculture

A new organization and policy approach came to Vermont in 1909 with the establishment of and appointment of a state commissioner of agriculture. The new Commissioner, Orlando Martin, a farmer and schoolmaster from Plainfield, Vermont, embraced a new approach that moved away from lectures the Board of Agriculture had used with farmer institutes. Instead, he promoted more public events such as Burlington's first annual farmer's week in cooperation with the State Agricultural College. He also established a "movable school of agriculture" with a special train loaned by the Rutland Railroad. The cars in the Rutland Special had exhibits on forestry and dairying horticulture and made demonstrations possible in the twenty-four places visited.[181] While this new educational approach was beneficial, establishing the federal extension service in 1914 supplied aid for more effective scholarly work in every county in the state at the local level with the farmers and their family members.[182]

Portrait of E. S. Brigham

In the *First Annual Report of the Commissioner of the Vermont Department of Agriculture* in 1909, E. S. Brigham, a farmer and future commissioner from St. Albans, presented a paper entitled "The Outlook for Vermont Farming." In the paper he extolled the virtues of cooperation and described how such organized efforts were working successfully for farmers in many places—even in Vermont with the apple growers of South Hero. The rural telephone and rural mail service, he stated, have "brought us closer together and given us better opportunities to exchange our thoughts."[183]

In 1913, after becoming commissioner, he stated that he was appointed with, "The definite understanding that the resources of this office were in a measure to be turned to the assistance of the farmers of Vermont in the marketing of farm products." He went on to say that, "The ultimate solution of the question of marketing farm products lies in the formation of cooperative farmers organizations . . . . The resources of this department will, in so far as possible, be given in the forming of such organizations."[184]

The first step, he argued, was the need for, "An enactment of a law similar to the laws of Massachusetts, New York, and Wisconsin, defining how an association or society, which calls itself co-operative shall be organized."[185]

Brigham brought in trained marketing specialists to help producers and creameries in the state.[186] By 1914 a few companies sold forty percent or more of the milk in New York, Chicago, Boston, Detroit, and other cities. Smaller dealers often followed price leads from these large operations, diminishing individual producers' economic leverage. Herbert Hoover, then United States Food Administrator, formed a producer-consumer commission to determine ways to provide fair pricing. Under an agreed-upon plan in the Boston market, dairy producers were to receive a fixed price plus a reasonable profit for milk. Any excess beyond market needs would result in a residual or surplus price to producers. A milk administrator was appointed to police the plan. This was quickly dismantled after WWI, but the mechanisms they worked out would become the foundation for massive intervention in the industry after 1933.[187]

The Commissioner of Agriculture was not alone in supporting the formation of agricultural cooperatives. Others were visionary in their analysis of the dairy situation. R. M. Washburn, a professor of dairy husbandry at the University of Vermont, felt that the growth of the cities would force Vermont to become a fluid milk state, and that cheese and butter factories would be closed down for lack of support.[188] He too felt that only by forming farmer cooperatives would the buyers in the city pay attention and offer a fair price for milk.

As evidence of the challenges presented to small farmers during this time, New England continued to experience a decrease in the number of farms in operation and the number of cows in the region, largely due to unattractive returns.

The Roots of Cooperation

The model for cooperative movement in the United States came primarily from Europe, and the heritage that many of the early settlers brought with them. Often cited are the Rochdale Cooperative (weavers) and the resulting Rochdale cooperative principles, the primary ones being "member-owned, member-controlled, and for member benefit."[189] These principles and the development of U.S. cooperatives are rooted in the upheavals that characterized the Industrial Revolution in England during 1750–1850. Accordingly, it is stated that dairy cooperatives were among the first types of agricultural cooperatives organized in the U.S., with the first creamery being built in Goshen, Connecticut in 1810. The trip to Europe in 1913 by the American and U.S. Commission of which Vermonter Charles Otis Gill was a part only reinforced this need for cooperation as the Commission brought back models of European Cooperatives of future value to farmers in the U.S.[190]

The cooperative model took several forms in the U.S. and even in Vermont. According to this history, in the mid-1840 Protective Unions were organized in Vermont by Wooster Sprague of Montpelier. These Unions provided insurance benefits and pension plans, and cooperative purchasing of food and supplies. It is said that by the time the movement broke up in 1857, there had been 152 unions or union stores in 129 Vermont towns.[191] It is stated that this movement paved the way for other active approaches, including:

- Vermont Dairymen's Association, founded in 1869

- Vermont Grange in 1872

- Vermont Maple Syrup Association of 1893

- Vermont Horticultural Society in 1895

- Union Agricultural Council (a federation of the Dairymen's, Maple Syrup, and Horticultural Associations) in 1935

- The Shoreham Cooperative Apple Producers Association in 1949

- Milk Producers Union in the Boston area from 1886–1911

- Boston Cooperative Milk Company founded in 1908

- New England Milk Producers Association or NEMPA, the most successful

- Vermont Cooperative Creameries Inc of 1920

The Grange movement, followed by the Farm Bureau, became important agents of change in the state and nationally by the late 1800s and early 1900s, and advocates for cooperatives. In fact, the Farm Bureau was recognized during this period as:

> The Agency through which the State Agricultural College and the USDA cooperate in all extension work in the county . . . and through the Farm Bureau the machinery for bringing the assistance of the county agent, the home demonstration agent, the county club leader, the extension specialist, the Agricultural College, the Experiment Station, and the USDA exist to address the most important problems in the community and how the work can best be done.[192]

This type of cooperation would be essential in advancing the cooperative system and agriculture within the state.[193]

National Cooperative Policy

Even with the passage of state laws promoting the advancement of cooperatives, much still needed to be done nationally. The Sherman Antitrust Act of 1890 broke up Standard Oil and other monopolies, and the Clayton Act of 1914 authorized labor unions and collective bargaining and sanctioned the establishment of cooperatives, both important progress. But there were still court cases against cooperatives. As a result, "In 1916, dairy marketing organizations, who felt they were being singled out for antitrust enforcement, formed the National Cooperative Milk Producers Association to solidify their strength and protect their general interests. Shortly thereafter, the Milk Producers joined with the National Grange, the National Farmers Union, and other farm organizations to form the National Board of Farm Organizations, headquartered in Washington, DC. For the first time, cooperative supporters had a unified voice in the Nation's Capital."[194] The Capper-Volstead Act was passed in 1922 as a result of this coordinated, national approach. Considered "the gold standard of farmer cooperative law," [Capper-Volstead] provided limited antitrust protections for farmer cooperatives, and enabled farmers to join together and collectively set prices for their products.

The Cooperative Era

Following the passage of the Capper-Volstead Act, it was said that, "At the present time nearly everyone from President Coolidge down is talking of co-operative marketing as a cure for the ills which American agriculture is heir to."[195]

The farmer cooperative model became the venue for addressing better and fairer pricing to farmers both for the products they raised and sold as well as for inputs for production. The interest in and establishment of cooperatives spread nationally, regionally, and within Vermont.

United Farmers' Co-Operative Creamery

In the eleventh Biennial Report of the Commissioner in 1920-22, thirty-two cooperative creameries were said to be operating since 1915, and nine had started operations since 1920.[196] This was seen as the marketing solution for Vermont's dairy sector, then the most important branch of agriculture in the state.

As reported by the state field agent in marketing, "To market these products in an orderly and efficient manner constitutes one of the largest marketing problems. These problems are being slowly solved through the creation and growth of the farmer-owned cooperative creamery associations." He went on to say that, "The next step in the cooperative plan is to join all of the cooperative creameries in the state into one cooperative organization or federation. Competition in marketing can be successfully met through the equal quality of products which can be rendered through consolidation."[197]

Vermont milk bottling

To address the marketing challenges to the state's dairy industry, now the most prominent and economically important agricultural sector of the time, attempts were made in the 1920s in New England to create one central marketing agency among the dairy farmer cooperatives—the same entities established to bargain with milk buyers for fairer pricing. Congress had given farmer cooperatives explicitly limited exemption from antitrust with the passage of the Capper-Volstead Act in 1922. This Act clarified the legal status of farmer cooperative marketing associations that had been challenged for antitrust behavior before the enactment of this Act. Even though the Boston milk market had implemented a classified pricing system as early as the 1890s (in which farmers receive a price based upon how handlers use the milk), three problems existed: no legal way existed for dairy farmers or their cooperatives to audit to assure the accuracy of use; no enforcement provisions required all handlers to abide by such a system; and there was no way to extend the system to non-farmer cooperative members. Since the Boston market received about seventy-five percent of the milk and cream shipped out of the State of Vermont, there was a great deal of concern about fair pricing by farmers and their support organizations. The 1929 stock market crash and Depression added urgency to this concern about adequate dairy farm pricing in Vermont and throughout the United States.

Other branches of agriculture in the state were becoming interested in cooperatives. Again, the field agent for marketing for the state was tasked with assistance, including the Marketing Committee of the maple products producers in the organization of the Vermont Maple Products Cooperative Exchange, Inc.[198] In the Thirty-Fourth Annual Report of the Vermont Maple Sugar Makers' Association, one of the speakers, H. C. Comings stated that, "As the years have gone by, it has seemed necessary to establish co-operative marketing associations in order to maintain a fair price for farm products both maple and dairy products. Co-operative marketing on sound business principles is the salvation of the Vermont farmers today." He went on to say that he agreed with a speaker at a meeting of the New England Council held in Burlington that "one of the best things our agricultural colleges could do would be to establish a course of training for business management of co-operative marketing. The crying need of Vermont today is business management in co-operative marketing."[199]

Franklin County Creamery Association

Cooperatives in Vermont and within the region continued to grow during the 1920s and 1930s, spurred by the support of the Grange, Farm Bureau, Extension, and the USDA with the passage of the Cooperative Marketing Act of 1926. The list of local cooperatives includes many like the Granite City Cooperative Creamery organized in 1920 by a group of local farmers; the Cabot Farmers' Cooperative established in 1919 when a group of 94 local farmers joined together to market milk; the Richmond Creamery formed in 1916 when thirty farmers began delivery of milk to the newly formed cooperative which became one of the most successful and well-regarded dairy cooperatives in Northern Vermont. Others include the St. Albans Cooperative Creamery in 1919, the Bellows Falls Cooperative Creamery in 1921, and in 1939 Northern Farms, which began as Green Mountain Dairies Cooperative, formed to help H. P. Hood Co. bargain on behalf of those shipping milk to Hood. At one time it was the largest farmer-member-owned dairy cooperative operating within Vermont. The Shoreham Apple Cooperative was formed in 1946, and many others were formed before and since.

Regional Initiatives

Barre Dairy and Ice Cream

Cooperation took place on the regional level, as well. In 1918, Horace A. Moses, a Massachusetts industrialist "took the lead in fostering the idea that a cooperative could be the means to make eastern farming more profitable." This led to the incorporation of the Eastern States Farmers' Exchange, a farmer-member cooperative for production of input supplies and services.[200] Another important regional initiative during this time was the establishment of the Eastern States Exposition. This was a concept advanced by some of the same individuals behind the Exchange, including Horace Moses. These individuals—led then by Joshua L. Brooks, a respected industrialist and agriculturalist—understood that:

> A reshuffling of the nation's economy introduced industry, commerce, and manufacturing as dominant forces along the Atlantic seaboard as well as strong agrarian competition from Western states which threatened to eclipse older Eastern farms in existence for several generations. The early 20th-century farmers faced issues unknown to their fathers and grandfathers in this new era of competing markets, more extensive transportation routes, and advancing technology. If the farmer fails to adopt the resources of both science and business, he cannot hold his own.[201]

The group concluded in their assessment that state boundaries needed to be set aside to address a common cause and common needs to better sustain agriculture and farming in the New England states. Out of this came the Eastern States Exposition, which first opened in 1916.[202]

George Aiken, Champion of Cooperatives

Vermont's governor George Aiken extolled the benefits of cooperatives in his book, *Speaking from Vermont*, in 1938. Governor Aiken would go on to serve as a U.S. Senator from 1942 through 1974, where he remained a champion of cooperatives. In Chapter IV, "Unless We Are Cooperative," he expressed the reasons for cooperation at all levels, from farm marketing and grading, insurance, financing, and purchasing. He wrote, "So agriculture today finds a very definite challenge to solve such problems as how to increase quality; how to lower production costs; how to maintain markets by reducing the spread between the farm and the consumer; how to create a new market for new products; how to maintain a high standard of living; how to use the land that came out of production; how to educate young people to farm; and how to maintain or increase our influence in the sphere of government."[203] Senator Aiken's influence on agriculture and rural life would be profound during his time in the U.S. Senate, where he served as a member of the Senate Committee on Agriculture.

New England Quality

While cooperation became the definitive method for bringing better marketing success and financial benefits to farmers, grades and standards became important for the promotion of value to customers. The Director of Marketing for the State Department of Agriculture provided information on the importance of standards and grades in the marketing of agricultural products.

New England Quality Product label

Vermont began to provide a New England state regional label in the mid 1920s for Vermont agricultural products, "so that consumers will have a way of identifying products on the market . . . that they may attract and command the premium they have earned." The Director went on to say that the advantage of such a label was "the ability to place Vermont products in even competition with other similar products from other states where such competition has been found to be keen."[204]

Copy of the Label New England Quality Product

Vermont neither had a large enough population it could serve with all the various agricultural products it produced nor the ability to sell these products elsewhere without the ability to export them to more regional markets. Vermont required cooperation and association among its farmers in the marketing of their products. The cooperative model appealed to many as a way to address better pricing and better pricing on production inputs. Many of the leaders during these times recognized the change that needed to take place for this to happen. Farm organizations and the political and policy establishment appeared to be in line to allow this to take place during these years.

The intent of Agriculture Commissioner E. S. Brigham beginning in 1913 had been to address ways to bring the resources of the U.S. Department of Agriculture, newly formed in 1909, to the assistance of farmers in the marketing of farm products. To further that effort, he appointed jointly "with the federal office of markets of USDA an individual with vast experience and knowledge." That person, Mogens R. Tolstrup, was a native of Denmark, "educated in schools in that country and at the Iowa State College of Agriculture where he served as an instructor of dairying. He made a careful survey of the leading markets for Vermont products and found markets for products such as beans, potatoes, wool, maple sugar, syrup, etc. He also assisted the creameries working under cooperative agreement in finding better markets."[205] This effort of market analysis and marketing assistance would carry on into the future.

WWI and the Flood of 1927

Vermont was still an agricultural state in 1918, with about seventy-nine percent of the land of the state in agricultural use, with over thirty-thousand farms. About eighty-five percent of these farms had dairy cows; most produced and shipped milk to over two hundred local creameries and cheese factories within the state. These farms were reasonably self-sufficient in meeting their own food needs. More than one-third of the population was engaged in farming. Diversity of production on the farm was an economic strength, which became evident during the flu of 1918 and World War I. A close read of small farm practices in the 1920s indicates that maple sugaring was so closely associated with other lines of farming and that it was the difference between the success or the failure of these operations in many instances.[206, 207]

The World War I Years

During World War I, a great deal of work went on to supply the food needs of the war effort, including Victory Gardens and their personal use. A National War Garden Commission existed to encourage Americans to contribute to the war effort.[208] People responded by creating more than 5.2 million victory garden plots cultivated in 1918, and an estimated thirty thousand Vermont School children worked to increase the state's food production. The Vermont War Council also trained young men from sixteen through twenty years old at Camp Vail in Lyndonville to work on farms to replace those who went to war.[209] The county, state, and federal extension services also helped to bring innovation and technology to farmers and their families. The need to increase production on the farm to respond to war food needs was advocated by agricultural leaders during this time. J. L. Hills, dean of the College of Agriculture at UVM said during the war that there was more reason for farmers to push production than ever before as there was an unequal market in Northern New England ("New England imports three-fourths of its food supply; there is worldwide hunger; there is a patriotic call to do so; and farmers can now get a liveable wage.") His prediction of favorable prices to last after the war would not hold.[210]

The Flood of 1927

Much has been written about this period and the Flood of 1927.[211] There was not any advance warning system like today, nor any long-range radar, cell phones, TV, instant messaging, or Facebook. Not all rural towns had electricity. It had been a very wet October in Vermont, and on November 2, 3, and 4, two great storms collided over the state. One came from the Gulf of Mexico and the other from the Great Lakes; together they dropped up to nine inches of water on an already water-drenched land mass in a forty-five-hour period. In one comparison, it was the equivalent of, "One cubic mile of the Atlantic Ocean being deposited on the State." According to records, "In a single day, Vermont was deprived of all modern conveniences, mail, telegraph, telephones, lights, gas, piped water, highways, railroad connections. The State had been set back a Century."[212] My wife's grandfather, Dr. E. H. Bancroft, a noted veterinary and the leader of the Barre City Granite Cooperative, said of that day that in traveling from Burlington back to Barre, "To describe all the things I saw, and came in contact with, on that trip, would require many pages, but the tremendous destruction of property, the loss of human lives, the sorrow and tragedy of it all, are indelibly stamped on my memory. It seemed to me then that I could not expect to live long enough to see Vermont back again to the prosperous little State she was getting to be."[213]

There are many tragic stories from this period, and stories of heroism too. Neighbors helped neighbors, communities helped other communities, and strangers helped those in need. President Coolidge dispatched his Secretary of Commerce, Herbert Hoover, to the state, where he said, "I have seen the worst of Vermont but the best of its people." Federal assistance was requested and provided. The Red Cross took full responsibility for finding housing and medical relief. Some eight thousand Vermonters received food, shelter, and medical comfort. Over one million dollars came in from contributors in other states. New England banks pledged one million dollars in capital stock to guarantee low-interest loans to farms, businesses, and other industries. The state legislature appropriated eight million dollars for two hundred miles of new roads. Vermont officials were quick to cut red tape to deal with immediate needs.

Rebuilding Vermont and a Look to the Future

The flood created a spirited sense of partnership at all levels within Vermont. While work was immediate to repair infrastructure, there was a yearning to develop a vision and plans for the future, to use all the positive energy to move Vermont forward, building upon the strengths of the past but with an enlightened program. "The great flood of November 1927 and the magnificent response to the call for concerted effort awakened in Vermonters a fuller sense of their powers and gave them a new impulse felt for years to come."[214] Thus, in the spring of 1928, just six months after the flood, the Vermont Commission on Country Life was organized. Chaired by Ex-Governor Weeks (who had been raised on a Salisbury dairy farm and was Governor during the flood), it was the first time a group of Vermonters formally assessed the State of the State and planned for the future.

Funded by the Social Science Research Council and the Rockefeller Foundation, The Commission on Country Life's report was a plan for rural rejuvenation and development in Vermont, and thus a blueprint for the future. Its Executive Director was Henry C. Taylor, one of the noted national agricultural economists of the time. He later became the first Executive Director of the Farm Foundation.

Some three hundred Vermonters participated in the effort over three years. (My wife's grandfather, Dr. E. H. Bancroft, chaired the dairy committee). It was an in-depth and comprehensive assessment of all aspects of Vermont: people, soils and climate, agriculture, forestry, and the woodworking industry, summer residents and tourism, fish, game and the preservation of wildlife, land utilization, rural home and community life, recreation, medical facilities for rural people, education facilities for rural people, the care of those in need, rural government, and other topics. The report set the agenda for the next few decades. It is vital to note that while the final report, *Rural Vermont: A Program for the Future,* was released in 1931, it did not mention the depression that began in 1929. Nevertheless, its conclusions helped to establish the strategies for the future of the state.[215]

Some key findings and recommendations came out of this very aggressive report, *Rural Vermont: A Program for the Future,* prepared by The Vermont Commission on Country Life.[216]

- Contribution of foreign-born: According to the census of 1930, foreign-born persons and persons one or both of whose parents were foreign-born make up nearly 30 percent of our farm population. The report said that members of forty-five farm families in Barre work in the stone sheds; of these, thirty-six belong to the foreign-born group. In this way, our foreign-born farmers furnish a part of the labor for specialized industries. They take up farms that would otherwise be abandoned, keep the land active, and enlarge the market for local merchants.

- Vermont's success in the past has depended on, and still relies on, turning the grass that grows on her meadows and pastures into the highest-priced salable product. The river valley soils are excellent farming lands, and some of Vermont's best dairy farms are located there. The hill areas of the stage are too rough and inaccessible to sustain prosperous agriculture. However, narrow valleys form small regions of good land. Dairying seems likely to continue to be the leading Vermont farm enterprise.

- The major dairy problems confronting Vermont farmers are low cost of production to meet competition, adjustment of supply to demand, and efficient marketing. What is needed is a cohesive organization of producers dealing with a coherent organization of city dealers, creating equality of bargaining power between the two groups. The report finds in the recommendations from the dairy committee that the outlook for the industry is promising provided that the industry develops and maintains a robust program: 1, to keep down the cost of production; 2, to bring about close adjustment to demand in both quality and seasonal distribution; and 3, to develop a more efficient marketing procedure.

- Apples, principally McIntosh, are not an acute apple marketing problem but an essential income source in specific communities and confident individuals. At the time, there were some 5,000 acres with about 325,000 trees. The leading variety was McIntosh, and the type made the product sale a simple matter. The report indicated that the state has no acute apple marketing problem.

- Maple sugar and syrup production is a material source of income on many Vermont farms; over ½ have sugar bushes. The production of maple products has an essential place in the future development of Vermont's agricultural program, especially on marginal farms where the land is ill-suited to ordinary crop production.

- Potatoes were then a growing but minor enterprise in the state. Anyone contemplating engaging in a commercial business should carefully consider what acreage will justify the purchase of planting, spraying, and harvesting equipment. Probably more potatoes are annually moved into than are forced out of the state.

- The state should expand and extend the scope of the Vermont State Bureau of Publicity. The money spent should be considered an investment rather than an expenditure. With the Extension Service, work should continue educating owners of tourist homes in the fundamentals of the tourist business.

- Improving highways as rapidly as possible is an essential feature of recreational development. A scenic road, well up on the slopes of the Green Mountains, into a system of scenic highways should be established, which is one of the most notable scenic highways of the U.S.

- It ought to be possible for Vermont farmers, or groups of farmers, to supply to camps, cottages, and hotels vegetables and fruits that may be produced within our borders so that they will not be necessary to be sent to metropolitan markets. Also, roadside stands should be limited to products grown by Vermont farmers or groups of farmers and should not be allowed to become commercialized organizations that do not maintain a close connection with local farms and things compete with the regularly established stores and markets.

- Recommend that the state take over the principal mountains' summits as rapidly as possible for park and forestry purposes. Everything possible should be done to call the attention of city dwellers to the opportunities Vermont offers for summer residences. This does not mean that we displace our productive farms with a non-agricultural class of residents, but rather that we should utilize the areas where the scenery is beautiful. The soil is not very fertile. A special effort should be made to interest possible purchasers of summer homes in what Vermont offers in this respect.

- The state should assume responsibility for the solution of the hill town problem as the economic difficulties of the hill farmers have become more severe with recent trends in agricultural production. Further study of the situation in each town is necessary, and a program and plan for the economic development in each hill town should be formulated. Recommend that a permanent state land utilization commission be set up of the State Forester, Ag Commissioner, an ag economist from the Land Grant, and others chosen to represent industry and recreation interests.

- We should keep our state free from crude and offensive advertising signs, from cheap and vulgar displays along the roadside, and from all that world offend good taste. Vermont will spread far and wide for the loveliness as a vacation state.

- It is recommended that a survey be made of our streams to ascertain the degree of and remedy for pollution. No one should have a right to pollute a stream, nor to deposit garbage, filth, germ carriers, or any other waste matter on public highways, in parks and other public property, or on the private premises of his neighbors. Pollution can be prevented, and the writing is already effective and informative. Still, one suggestion could be to include more specific examples or anecdotes to illustrate further the points being made. Additionally, including more information on the impact of these changes on the everyday lives of farmers and consumers could make the writing more engaging. Finally, breaking up the longer paragraphs into smaller chunks could make reading and digesting the information easier. The damage of the past can be partially overcome.

This progressive report, *Rural Vermont: A Program for the Future,* in 1931, helped to set goals and objectives for the state. The New Deal period that came about with the election of a new president would intersect with many of the recommendations made in this report and would be issues that would confront the state well into the future.

Vermont was one of only six states which voted to re-elect embattled Republican incumbent Hoover, and would be one of only two states that would reject FDR in all four of his presidential campaigns. Vermont was the most Republican state in the nation.[217] And it was against this background that President Franklin Roosevelt was elected President, and the New Deal programs of his administration came into being.

The New Deal would bring new policy approaches to agriculture and farming. According to a review of the policies, "A majority of Vermonters, who strongly identified with the Republican Party, didn't support the Democratic Roosevelt administration, but some New Deal programs were welcomed. Vermonters willingly accepted programs that put them back to work but were wary of major projects that involved loss of local control to the federal government."[218]

CHAPTER EIGHT

The New Deal

SOME FELT THAT THE IMPACT OF THE GREAT DEPRESSION on the Vermont farm sector was better than in other parts of the United States due to its agricultural diversity and the ability of farmers to grow their own food."[219] Vermont legislative leader George Aiken said, "Here we are, most of us healthy and well-nourished, comfortably warm and self-supported—'statistically bankrupt.'"[220]

Still, Vermont lost about 1,500 out of 25,000 farms during the Depression, and income from the sale of milk, Vermont's most important agricultural product, fell by half from 1929 to 1933. At the time, dairy products comprised roughly 65 percent of Vermont's agricultural income. Other important products included apples, potatoes, chickens, maple, turkeys, small fruits and vegetables, beef, cattle, and meats; but dairy was economically the most important.

According to the *Story of Vermont*, "Agriculture in mid-twentieth-century Vermont was drastically different from agriculture a century earlier. By 1930, nearly 75 percent of Vermont farms were categorized as specialized (meaning that one product accounted for more than 40 percent of farm income), mainly in dairy. Some 6 percent of farms in the State were self-sufficient. One hundred years before, nearly all farms were virtually self-sufficient. As Vermont farms became increasingly connected to larger market forces, small self-sufficient farms disappeared."

In the personal report of the Commissioner of Agriculture E. H. Jones in 1932, he said that the economic conditions of farmers were not good:

> The last twelve months has been an extremely trying time for Vermont farmers. In this process of economic readjustment, much of the merchandise they were obliged to purchase remained at inflated values. At the same time, the commodities they sell are subject to prices greatly reduced. Interest, taxes, and other fixed charges of farm operation have remained the same as in periods of prosperity. In contrast, the purchasing power of the farmer's dollar has diminished to approximately one-half of its former value. Under these conditions, it is challenging and impossible for them to meet their obligations.[221]

Vermont voted for Herbert Hoover over Roosevelt in the election of 1932, 57.66 percent to 41.08 percent. Vermont was a bastion of liberal Northeastern Republicanism; by 1932 the Green Mountain State had gone Republican in every presidential election since the founding of the Republican Party. Hoover had come to Vermont representing President Coolidge during the 1927 flood to survey the damage. He had also brought some initial stability for dairy pricing in the Boston market in the early 1920s as the federal Food Administrator under President Coolidge.

It was not surprising then that when the New Deal was created, there was some skepticism to this form of federal activism including from leaders like George Aiken, a legislator in Vermont at the time and a noted farmer and agriculturist. However, many New Deal initiatives benefitted Vermont farmers: "Rural Electric, subsidized lime and fertilizers, subsidized credit, milk market orders, and classified pricing were essential to the development and survival of Vermont agriculture."[222] New Deal programs would have a profound impact on Vermont agriculture, lasting into the modern era.

Before the New Deal

The passage of the New Deal programs was a significant change in the federal farm policy agenda. In an assessment of New Deal programs' impact on farming practices, Dr. Don Paarlberg of Purdue University wrote that, "For 70 years, after the passage of the Morrill Act, which set up the Land Grant Colleges, the farm policy agenda had been agricultural development; the components of that policy were research, classroom teaching, on-farm education, and improvement of agricultural resources."[223, 224]

The 1920s was a period of severe financial conditions in the farm sector, especially at the national level. Increased agricultural production had occurred during the war, but demand decreased after food exports declined. This production increase and decrease resulted in a sharp drop in farm prices, a 56% decline from 1929–1932 in the index of farm prices.[225]

Widespread government intervention in the farm economy began in 1929, when President Herbert Hoover created the Federal Farm Board as part of the Agricultural Marketing Act of 1929. Hoover had served as Federal Wartime Food Administrator and had supported the Capper-Volstead Act under President Harding. He also provided leadership at the Federal Wartime Food Administration, with an initiative to stabilize the Boston fluid milk market during World War I. He supported farmer cooperatives and saw the solution as glutted markets that cooperatives could best address. Vermont and New England had embraced the farmer cooperative movement as a way to bring new technology and economic viability to the economy of the region.

While President Hoover recognized the need for intervention to bring about better farm pricing, the provisions of the Agricultural Marketing Act failed to achieve their desired purposes. The AMA promoted cooperatives (in 1926, a division of cooperative marketing was created within USDA), and the federal Board had eight members representing the primary farm cooperatives in the U.S. The law intended to have the cooperatives control the production of crops and to increase exports as a way to better pricing.[226] The Board had $500 million from the U.S. Treasury to carry out its activities. To increase dairy pricing, for example, the Board lent Land O'Lakes Dairy Cooperative to withhold butter sales and purchase additional product from the market. The Board also organized a dairy program with five regional butter-marketing associations to aid dairy cooperatives in production controls and marketing. It was suggested that the federal government would pay farmers to reduce the size of their herds to cut surplus dairy products. This voluntary effort by farmers to cut production implemented through the farmer cooperatives failed to produce the desired results. (Farmers are an independent bunch, and when prices are low producer response tends to be to produce as much as possible, even though this does not benefit the industry as a whole.) Prices continued to decline, and Treasury funds were depleted. However, this experiment on voluntary approaches to production controls coordinated by farm cooperatives set the stage for new farm legislation within the first 100 days of the Roosevelt Administration.[227]

The Agricultural Adjustment Act

With the failure of voluntary approaches through cooperatives to address declining farm prices, there was an increased urgency among farm organizations for more direct federal intervention. President Roosevelt asked his Secretary of Agriculture Henry Agard Wallace to assemble farm leaders to reach a consensus on what could be done.[228] A well-organized farm-lobbying group developed the centerpiece of the New Deal, which aimed to return the agricultural market to the good prices that had prevailed from 1909 to 1914.[229,230]

The 1933 Agricultural Adjustment Act, one of President Franklin Roosevelt's First-One Hundred-Days initiatives, allowed farmers to enter into agreements with the Secretary of Agriculture to reduce their acreage or production in what was deemed to be seven essential commodities: wheat, cotton, corn, rice, tobacco, hogs, and milk. In return, farmers would receive payments derived from taxes levied on processors. Better compliance with classified pricing in markets like Boston was addressed by issuing federal licenses to milk dealers.

The Agricultural Adjustment Act was challenged immediately, and in the case of The U.S. vs. Butler, the Supreme Court found 6 to 3 that many provisions of the Act were unconstitutional based on the fact that they were an encroachment upon the rights of the states and that it was illegal to tax one group (processors) to support another (farmers). There were significant divisions on the Court regarding the opinion and the Roosevelt Administration moved quickly to overcome legal obstacles (including trying to pack the Court with its supporters). The Agricultural Marketing Act of 1937 provided apparent authority for federal marketing orders. It reaffirmed the marketing agreement provisions of the 1933 Act. Instead of taxing processors to support farmers, general funds were used. President Roosevelt indicated at a press conference in 1936 that "the answer to the farmer situation is production controls coupled with soil conservation." He emphasized that he was responsible for treating farming as a national problem.[231, 232]

Vermont and New England Dairy Farmers' Interest in the 1937 Act

In June of 1937 a conference of dairy leaders from four New England States including Vermont, organized by the governors of those states, unanimously adopted a resolution approving the federal control of dairy pricing.[233] The resolution described those states' power of the milk shed as being impossible because of interstate commerce laws. Most of the milk and cream going to Boston and surrounding cities came from states outside Massachusetts, so controls could not be imposed. This was due to the Commerce Clause of the U.S. Constitution.

George Aiken on the Capital steps

Governor George Aiken described the dire economic situation facing Vermont dairy farms (approximately 10,000 at that time). He said that federal control of milk pricing would save hundreds of dairy farmers in the state. The same year, when Congress debated the 1937 Agricultural Marketing Act, Governor Aiken sent a terse telegram to Capitol Hill: "Informed that the Senate was stalled on a procedural issue," Governor Aiken wrote in true New England style, "Dairy industry in peril, act without delay."[234]

Before 1937, Aiken's predecessor, Governor Charles Smith, had also expressed concern, saying that if the action were not taken to overturn a Court injunction prohibiting the federal government from enforcing key provisions of the federal license to milk dealers for classified pricing, the Boston market would crumble. There would, Smith and others predicted, be a disastrous effect on the interstate and intrastate commerce in milk and cream from Vermont.[235] Governor Aiken said in his farewell address to the Vermont legislature, "State officials and several farmer cooperatives appealed for a federal marketing order. As sufficient farmers voted, it went into effect and has led to the stabilization of milk prices in Boston, and later the New York milk shed."[236]

The Vermont Commission on Country Life report in 1931 indicated that "the major dairy problems confronting Vermont farmers are low cost of production to meet competition, adjustment of supply to demand, and efficient marketing."[237]

There continues to be a great deal of history around federal milk marketing orders that exist today and regulate most of the milk marketed in Vermont. These orders started in 1933 and since then have been, "mended, terminated, challenged in Courts, tinkered by Congress, debated, discussed and cursed."[238] The problems identified in the 1932 Report by the Country Life Commission continue to confront the dairy industry in Vermont up to the present day.

Other Key New Deal Legislation
Farm Credit Act of 1933

The Farm Credit Act provided funding to refinance one-fifth of farm mortgages over eighteen months. It also established local Production Credit Associations throughout the U.S. and twelve District Banks for Cooperatives with one Central Bank for Cooperatives (Federal Land Banks in the twelve Districts had been created by federal law in 1916).

The Farm Credit Administration was established as an independent agency by Executive Order. (Henry Morgenthau, later Secretary of Treasury, a dairy farmer and fruit grower from Dutchess County, New York, was appointed Chairman of the Federal Farm Credit Board and Governor of the Farm Credit Administration. He had chaired the New York Agricultural Advisory Committee when Roosevelt was Governor of the state.[239]) Significant amendments to the Farm Credit Act in 1987 resulted in changes in the organizational structure of these farmer-owned institutions as initially established by Congress. They remain a farmer- and cooperatively-owned lending institution in the United States and the Northeast. In Vermont, they are now part of Farm Credit East. (Note: President Teddy Roosevelt's Country Life commission had recommended a cooperative credit system for farmers). Also, Charles Otis Gill, a Vermonter, was appointed by Vermont's Governor to serve as a member of the commission that studied European models of cooperatives in 1913, resulting in the 1916 passage of the first Farm Credit Act which created the Federal Farm Loan Bank. In his book, *Speaking from Vermont*, George Aiken said that he helped start one of the three Production Credit Associations that do business in Vermont.[240]

Rural Electric Administration

In 1935, President Roosevelt signed an executive order creating the Rural Electric Administration (REA). At that time, only twelve percent of U.S. farms had electric service, as it was not economically advantageous for large electric companies to string lines in rural areas. Electricity changed life both on the farm and in the home. Farms no longer needed ice houses for cooling milk and could use machines for milking their cows. Electricity could light the barns instead of oil lamps. Homes could have electricity and pumped water, and eventually bathrooms with pumped water and toilets instead of outhouses.

As a point of interest, I asked my 95-year-old mother if she remembered when they were provided electricity in Brookline, Vermont. She said, "Yes, the year was 1938, and your father was farming with his father, and they brought one line into the house, and we had one

15-watt bulb. I told your father, that is bright, and we will never need anything brighter."

Soil Conservation and Domestic Allotment Act

Congress passed the Soil Conservation and Domestic Allotment Act in 1936 in response to the dust bowl that swept the West.[241, 242] The Act established a policy for addressing soil erosion, creating the Soil Conservation Service (or SCS, now the National Resource and Conservation Service) under the USDA. To increase the functionality of this new agency, Roosevelt decided local input should be a part of this mix. In 1937 Roosevelt asked all state governors to promote model state legislation to allow the formation of Soil Conservation Districts within the state as a partner with SCS.[243]

These Districts were established by Vermont law in 1939 and still exist. With their members, the local Soil and Water Conservation Districts have the authority under state law, working in partnership with NRCS to address soil and water conservation issues. Districts, and their boards of elected supervisors, were given a variety of powers including the ability to conduct surveys, investigations and research relating to the character of soil erosion and prevention, to conduct demonstration projects in order to demonstrate by example the means, methods, and measures by which soil erosion can be prevented and controlled, and to carry out measures for the prevention and control of soil and stream bank erosion and the protection and conservation of natural resources among other powers.

This law has been altered, amended, and changed numerous times since it was created. However, much of the original wording remains because the focus and purpose of local conservation districts has remained the same. The law clearly identifies the need to conserve all renewable natural resources through the voluntary actions of Vermont residents.

Resettlement Administration

The Resettlement Administration was created in 1935 with three primary purposes: (1) loans and grants to needy farmers; (2) erosion, flood control, and land retirement; and (3) resettlement programs.[244]

One of the proposals for Vermont was the retirement of 20,000 acres of marginal "hill country" land and permanent placement into forestry. The goal was to turn underproductive farms into tree farms and parks.

There was a great deal of division on the subject, with George Aiken opposed (loss of local control that would hinder the development of the state), and other notable figures like author and educator Dorothy Canfield Fisher, Commissioner of Agriculture Ed Jones, leaders of the State Grange, and Chamber of Commerce were in support.

Then-Governor Wilson appointed a committee to select the land for retirement. The conditions laid down by the Committee for an agreement were too demanding for the federal government, and it withdrew its offer.[245] The state legislature in 1935 had enacted a law authorizing the purchase of submarginal land by the federal government with the consent of the Land Use Board safeguarding the rights and sovereignty of the state and the people of the state. George Aiken was the Chair of the Land Use Board at the time and he determined that the conditions laid down by the federal government for the purchase of about 50 percent of the land area of the state were not acceptable.[246]

Wellman's Farm, view of Osgood Farm in the background

The loss of hillside farms continued to be a significant issue facing Vermont. In 1931, the Vermont Commission on Country Life had recommended that. "The state should assume the responsibility for the solution of the hill town problem as the economic difficulties of the hill farmers have become more severe with recent trends in economic production. It further found that most of the land in hill towns is submarginal from an agricultural production standpoint.[247]

The Resettlement Administration was replaced by the Farm Security Administration, which became the Farmers' Home Administration in 1946. Much later, Federal farm lending and crop support programs were to be handled in Vermont and the rest of the U.S. through the Farm Service Agency ("FSA"). The Farm Service Agency was created by reorganizing USDA agencies in the 1990s. A County Committee and State Committee structure was established to guide and support activities of the programs within each state FSA. The Federal Crop Insurance Corporation, now the Federal Risk Management Agency, was created and renamed in 1996.

Agricultural Stabilization and Conservation Service

During the 1940s, the Agricultural Stabilization and Conservation Service ("ASCS") replaced the Agricultural Adjustment Administration ("AAA") in administering federal laws related to agriculture. The ASCS had regional, state, and county offices of which Vermont was a part. As was the case under the AAA, each county had a farmers' committee working in cooperation with federal employees.[248] The mission of the ASCS was to promote conservation and price stability. Every county in Vermont had its own county ASCS office. Services included distributing price-support payments and cost-share programs for various conservation projects. In 1994, the ASCS was merged with other agriculture agencies to create the Farm Service Agency. This organization with the county and a state committee provided subsidized phosphorus and other products to Vermont farmers. Its impact was a way to bring local and state attention to the needs of working farms through federal financial support for soil and water conservation efforts in coordination with the state and Soil Conservation Service. Unfortunately subsidized phosphorus led to increased pollution of the rivers and streams of Vermont.

Entrance to the Parkway from Bennington-Brattleboro Road

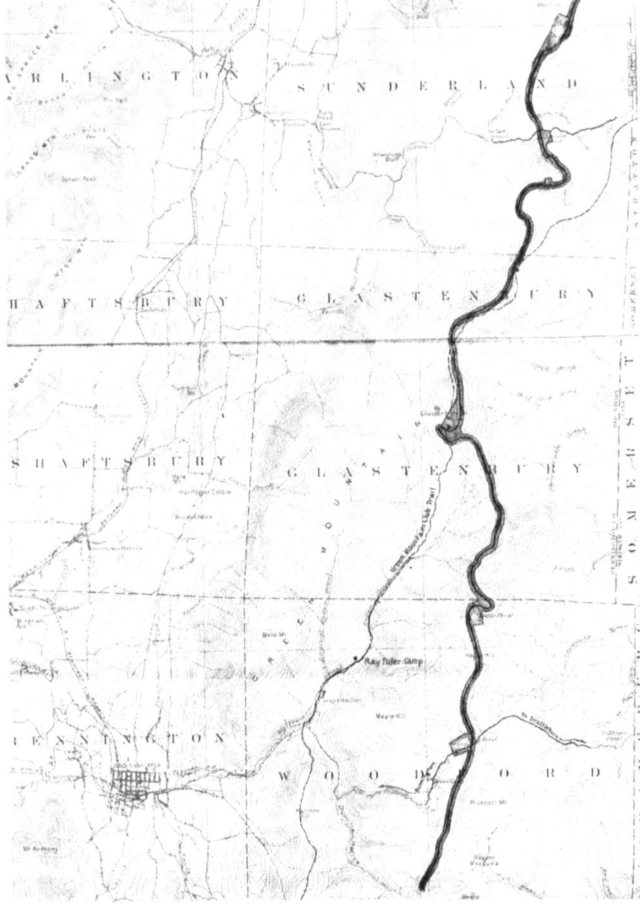

Green Mountain Parkway proposed route

Green Mountain Parkway Route survey map

Proposed Green Mountain Parkway

This Parkway that was planned to run the length of the state would be a sister to the Blue Ridge Parkway.[249] A scenic highway was not a new idea, as the Vermont Commission on Country Life had suggested in its report that "scenic highways, well up on the slopes of the Green Mountains, on either side of this range, constructed in semi-permanent form, would appeal strongly to lovers of beautiful scenery. Likewise, a similar policy might be followed in connecting the roads nearest to Lake Champlain in a system that would extend from the Canadian border to the Southern extremity of the lake, thus affording what might be made one of the most notable scenic highways of the United States."[250]

The report also recommended that the state "take over, as rapidly as possible, the summits of the principal mountains for park and forestry purposes."[251] "The Roosevelt administration offered $18 million in WPA funds to build the parkway, which was to emulate the Skyline Drive in Virginia, but after three years of argument and several hotly-contested hearings between 1933 and 1936, the proposal was rejected three times by the General Assembly. Eventually, the legislature called for a popular referendum."[252] Views for and against the building were very spirited and have been the subject of historical reviews.[253] A referendum was held on Town Meeting Day in 1936. The parkway proposal was soundly defeated, with 42,873 opposed versus 30,895 in support of the construction, even though referendums are not binding in Vermont.[254, 255]

Smugglers Notch from Mt. Mansfield route of the Green Mountain Parkway

CHAPTER NINE

After the New Deal

T HE FEDERAL NEW DEAL OF THE 1930s brought forth new programs and approaches to economic development nationally and within the State of Vermont.[256] Many of these programs were based around state and federal cooperation. The economy was also changing on the farm with electricity, mechanization, and the telephone. Laws and programs in the early 1900s encouraged the development of farmer cooperatives in marketing products and inputs for production.

UVM Agricultural College Fruit Show

Still, farmers struggled. The *Rutland Herald* in 1940 ran an article on the status of agriculture in the state.[257] The paper reported that "even social and political cycles in the past 15 years have brought Vermont a disastrous flood, a market crash, and several depressions, and FDR's reconstruction became a national catchword. Just as agriculture is the right bower of existence in the Green Mountains, so dairying is the backbone of the state's agriculture—dairy depression, as dairy suffered as people did not have enough money to buy milk. Farmers turned to other pursuits. It has been the best five years in the production of high-grade apples; the poultry business has grown by leaps and bounds, mink raising is a cash crop, well-to-do individuals are raising beef, cheese making continues, beekeeping takes place, submarginal lands are being sold as summer residences or planted to trees. The Extension Service is helping farmers plant more clover and alfalfa instead of corn. Maple continues to hold an important place in the State." The article concluded, "Nobody predicts the future of Vermont agriculture. But it is not for the lack of faith as a way of life. It is because high living does not result from agriculture returns."

The World War II years again brought about changes in the farm and the economy. Food and other supplies were rationed, and a labor shortage occurred as many able bodied men served. Prices for products from the farm were strong during the war but would decline again once it ended.

The landscape of Vermont agriculture continued to be challenged in the second half of the century, with the construction of the Interstate Highway System, grocery-store chains moving in to replace traditional milk delivery, legislative reapportionment that shifted political power from rural to more populated areas, and the eventual loss of the New Deal government regulation of milk pricing.

Eisenhower Interstate Highway System

The Interstate Highway System, constructed in Vermont in the late 1950s and 1960s, had a significant impact on the economy and landscape of the state just as the development of canals, railroads, and improved roads had done in the past. While a public referendum in 1936 defeated a proposed Green Mountain Parkway, no such significant opposition occurred to the federal Interstate proposal. The mood changed with the Cold War era. Vermont had approximately sixty-three thousand registered vehicles by 1955 instead of twenty-seven thousand in 1930. During World War II, the production of non-military cars for civilian use was discontinued in 1942 and began again when the war ended.

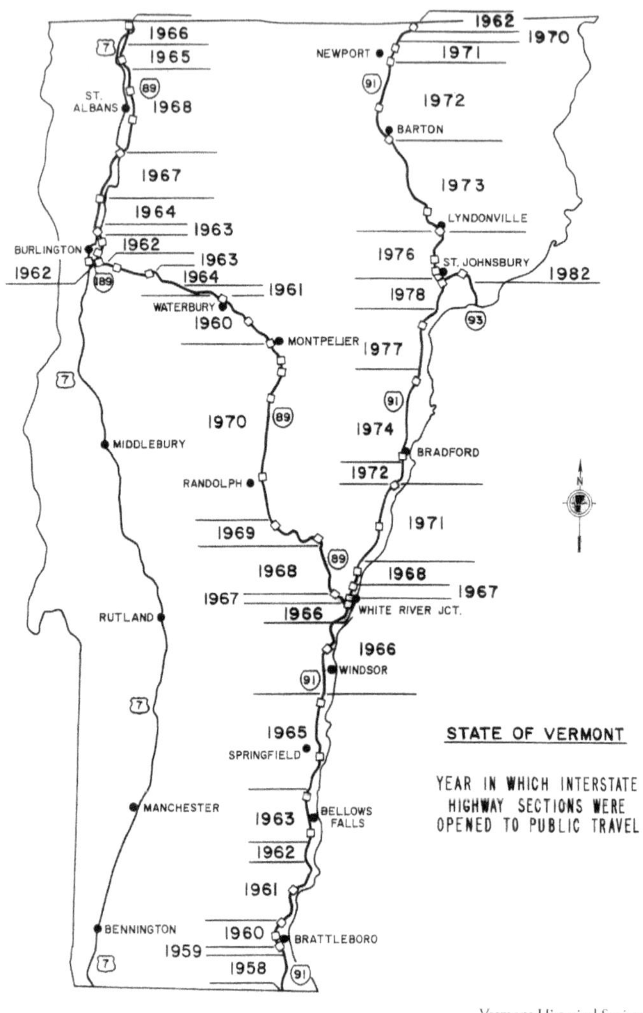

Vermont Historical Society

Map of the completion of the Vermont Interstate System

A report by Arthur Woolf, "The Impact of Interstate Highways 89 and 91 on Vermont's Economy and Demographics," found that the road had a profound impact on the economy and population growth in the state. On population, the U.S. census counted 343,000 residents in the state, a population nearly stagnated in the first half of the twentieth century. According to his report and census data however, in the 1960s, 70s, and 80s, Vermont's population grew faster than the nation's. The highway system further integrated Vermont into the national economy and increased access of tourists to the state.[258] In 1960, there were 18,000 seasonal homes in Vermont, and by 1980 the census counted 34,000, nearly double that which existed twenty years earlier.[259]

Some viewed the Interstate highway as a further erosion of many aspects of rural life in the state. Still, the change was happening regardless of this opposition. The State Board of Agriculture had aggressively advertised for selling Vermont abandoned farms in the late 1800s, for they recognized the value of tourism to the state, as did a 1932 "Study of the Future of Vermont" coming out of the 1927 flood.[260]

With the new interstate highway, Vermont officials launched a marketing campaign in the 1960s called, "The Beckoning Country."[261] Its purpose was to appeal to city dwellers in Boston and New York looking for an escape. Elbert Moulton, who held a variety of development posts in the state in a career that spanned several decades, said of the highway, "It took us out of the sticks and put us within a day's drive of 80 million people and right in the main economic stream of the country."[262] While the highway system increased access to markets and increased the flow of more distant food to consumers, the changes also further impacted the landscape and the economy of the state. In the book, *Farms, Flatlanders, and Fords: A Story of People and Place in Rural Vermont 1890-2010*, the author captures the changes in the close-knit community of North Pomfret. He writes that "The decline was not rapid, as men returned from World War II intent on continuing this occupation of farming. But market forces led to decreases in milk prices. With technological changes and new health and regulatory standards like the bulk tank, dairy farming has become unprofitable for many. With the advent of the automobile and improved roads, many could find employment elsewhere. The everyday community's social structure that had evolved around the towns' working dairy farms could no longer continue easily."[263]

Growth of Grocery Chains and the End of Home Milk Delivery

Records show that the home delivery of milk was a big business across the nation before the 1960s and the advent of regional supermarkets and refrigeration.[264] Many local milk bottlers and distributors existed in

Vermont at the time, and the variety of milk bottles indicates the extent of the delivery system.

It was common for farmers of the time to have a small home delivery route that served their community. For example, Orin Thomas started delivering milk in Rutland City in 1921, and Thomas Dairy was born. Richard James in Weybridge started Monument Farms Dairy, bottling milk in his basement in 1930.[265] Thomas Dairy closed in 2020, one of the last Vermont-owned dairy processors.[266] In Brattleboro in 1920, the Windham County Cooperative Milk Producers Association existed as a cooperative effort of 170 farmers delivering milk to the plant. The plant opened in 1921 and operated until 1946. Maple Farms Dairy was buying up many small operators in the area. The local operation was shut down in 1978, tipping the economies of scale in favor of larger regional dairy plants and the sale of milk at large grocery chains.[267]

According to USDA, home delivery was a mainstay in the 1950s, with one-half of milk delivered to the home, and by 2005 it was only 0.4%.[268] The post-World War II period of prosperity brought a boost in automobile ownership and the movement to the suburbs of the population. People became more mobile, and with the growth of supermarkets and refrigeration in the home and store, people could buy several items at once.[269] These stores had large refrigeration units, and articles could be stored and shipped over long distances and in larger units. Often this resulted in the inability to compete with local production. Milk, too, was sent longer distances in larger volumes to a processing facility. It was packaged into coated paper cartons and polyethylene containers, replacing the glass bottle patented in 1874.

Dr. Fred Webster, a Professor of Extension at the University of Vermont, said "when I came to UVM in 1956, there were 230 milk dealers in the State, and most did home deliveries. Going back to the 1920s and '30s, you could multiply that number by 10." In 1944, data indicates that 44% of Burlington and 45% of Essex, Vermont residents relied on the home delivery of milk.[270]

The Elimination of Milk Cans in Shipping Milk

Bottling milk, Vermont

Vermont milk cartons

The farm I grew up on in Brookline, Vermont and others nearby shipped their milk in 10-gallon cans cooled in water until the late 1950s and early 1960s. Many of the farms in the community had a few cows and sent the milk to nearby creameries. I remember vividly the milk truck pulling up to the farm and the driver pulling the cans from the water, putting them in the truck, and leaving clean cans behind. When the requirement came from the handlers that shipping milk would quire a bulk tank, many dairy farms in the state ceased production. Milk handlers saw this as a way to decrease their handling and shipping costs. But installing these new bulk tanks was costly. It required new milking facilities or a structure to hold the tank, which could have hundreds of gallons at a controlled temperature until the truck arrived. Keith Wallace, a Waterbury Dairy Farmer and President of the Vermont Farm Bureau, in a letter to Vermont dairy farmers, spelled out the results of a study based on the present prices of tanks, current prices of milk, present sizes of farms and herds and financial status of farmers in the state.[271] According to the analysis presented, "most of the experts agree that bulk tanks are feasible on herds of thirty or more cows and that their use is practical for very few Vermont dairymen. Information taken from the College of Agriculture Extension Service taken from town listers' reports showed that sixty percent of farms having 18 or fewer cows and eighty percent had 28 or less cows, and so tanks are not feasible but for a few dairy farms in the State of Vermont." In 1950, Vermont had nearly 11,000 dairy farms with an average herd of 25 cows. By 1963 Vermont had only one-third left; by 1970, two-thirds had ceased operation.[272] This change significantly impacted the rural community and the working landscape of the state. Before the bulk tank requirement, the small town of Brookline I grew up in had several farms shipping milk, including the farm I grew up on, and after the condition, only three dairy farms continued in the early 1960s.

The middle of the 20th century brought considerable changes to farming, including the dairy industry, with technological innovation, mechanization, and machinery allowing for increased production on the farm. Vermont hilltop farms would continue to lose their importance.[273]

Reapportionment of the Legislature in 1965

Until reapportionment in 1965, which was mandated by a 1964 Supreme Court ruling, the Vermont Constitution had upheld fair representation as one town, one vote. For example, Brookline, having a population of 500, had the same power as the City of Burlington, with a population of approximately 45,000. My grandfather, Gerald Allbee, was a Representative from Brookline before Reapportionment. As a part-time legislature that met every two years, it adjourned so its members, many farmers, could go home for Town meetings and sugaring season. With the passage of apportionment changes in 1965 that required equal representation, the size of the Vermont House of Representatives dropped overnight from 246 to 150. Rural expression in the Vermont House decreased, furthering and empowering the interests of more urban areas.[274] Before this time, the Vermont House of Representatives had always been the stronghold of farmer interests and had constituted the largest occupational group.[275] In his book *Dateline Vermont*, Chris Graff writes that, "Reapportionment in the House of Representatives in 1965 was the longest and most emotional battle ever fought in Vermont." Graff also quotes the late Emory Hebard, who chaired the special committee on Reapportionment and said in 1989, "Vermont ceased to be Vermont. It is one of the worst things we did to the State of Vermont; we lost something."[276]

It is difficult to predict what laws might have been passed if the legislature was not reapportioned, but local small-town voices are not as quickly heard as they were before.

Back to the Land Movement of the 1960s

At the same time as political power was shifting away from rural areas, a new social movement brought an influx of people to Vermont. Between 1960 and 1990, the state recorded the fastest expansion rate per decade since the 18th century, with an estimated 173,000 new permanent residents,[277] an almost 50 percent increase. The Vermont Historical Society has documented that, "The back-to-the-land movement of that time birthed the institutions that, in their maturity, made Vermont what it is today." A common thread among many new arrivals was self-sufficiency, as the first European settlers to the state were to grow food from the land with greater self-reliance, autonomy, and community.[278]

The work of journalist Dorothy Thompson in Bernard, Vermont in the 1940s to "promote country life and protect the family farm foreshadowed the 'Back-to-The-Land' movement by a good twenty years."[279] She was considered to be ahead of her time. She wrote, "The houses will fall in, and the villages which live from the farms will disappear, and all the comeliness that it is will be gone, and the future of other such communities seems to me a very high price to pay for a war of freedom: a grotesque price and a price that doesn't have to be paid if people would think and plan in another direction. I see the Land Corps as a specific help for that kind of farm and America, and that is why I am so passionately interested in it."[280]

The "Plowing Old Ground" exhibit focuses on Vermont's organic farming pioneers in the 1960s and 1970s[281] and can be found at www.cornucopia.org. Many consider the Back to The Land movement as the beginning of increased attention to more local food and organic production. In her book, *We Are as Gods: Back to the Land in the 1970s on the Quest for a New America*, Kate Daloz, who grew up on a farm in Glover, Vermont, says that this movement helped to propel the demand for organic food.[282] Many others, including Enid Wonnacott of NOFA-VT, and numerous other farmers throughout the state were leaders in establishing organic farming that continues.

How the Ski Industry Changed Vermont

The back-to-the-landers were not the only ones flocking to enjoy Vermont's hills. The midcentury period also saw the development of Vermont's ski industry.

The work of the late forester Perry Merrill is essential to the history of ski areas in the State of Vermont. According to "The Early Days of Skiing, 1934," in *Vermont History*, (at vermonthistory.org/early-days-of-skiing-1934) State Forester Perry Merrill used workers from the Civilian Conservation Corps, a New Deal initiative, to cut Vermont's first trails specifically for skiing and to build a parking site and warming shelter at Mt. Mansfield's Smuggler's Notch area. In 1939, Governor Aiken authorized at Mt. Mansfield the first lease of state-owned land to private

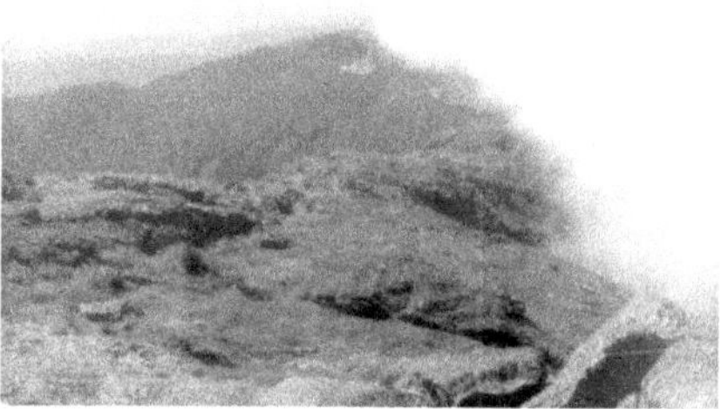

Chin of Mt. Mansfield
- Long Trail Photos

Hikers on Mt. Mansfield
- Long Trail Photos

developers for ski area use. Aiken justified this commercial development of public land by asserting the state's need to balance environmental preservation and economic growth. A later governor, Deane Davis, would bring attention to uncontrolled development around ski areas that would result in the passage of Act 250 legislation in 1970 due to the Gibb Commission.[283]

Vermont had devoted considerable time and effort to promoting itself, and second homes began to be built on the slopes and sides of mountains, areas that could only support the housing with remedial measures. The Act addressed these environmental concerns along with the need to protect prime and significant agricultural land, which remain a part of the criteria that exist today.

According to state information, the ski industry in Vermont has about 4 million visitors annually, and 75% of those skiers are from out of state. The industry contributes about $1.6 billion to the state's economy each year. Along with direct revenues and indirect revenue from real estate development, the ski industry brought increased attention to the development of industry and business-related tourism in the state.

Gubernatorial Efforts for Farmers

Over time, various governors have tried to address ways to keep Vermont farms sustainable and economically viable. The list that follows is not complete but is intended to show that each Administration has tried to address ways to encourage and sustain a more viable agricultural sector as markets and conditions have changed. Governor's efforts include:

- Governor Aiken supported the development of farmer cooperatives.

- Governor Mortimer Proctor appointed two committees to formulate a progressive farm policy for the state in 1946. Their recommendations included the need for dairy farmers to reduce costs to be competitive; funding to the state agricultural college for facilities for research, instruction in processing and manufacturing of milk and milk products; and the establishment of a marketing authority with standards and an official label. The report also recommended a policy for Vermont that encourages the production of apples, maple products, potatoes, canning corn, and diversification.

- In his inaugural address in 1958, Governor Joseph Johnson said, "There is but one choice for Vermonters, and that is to put into effect a program which will sell the products Vermont agriculture can produce efficiently." He also said that his legislature and succeeding legislatures should, "Always work to purify our lakes and streams. Some good anti-pollution work has been done in Vermont. Still, there is much yet to be done."

- Governor Philip Hoff's agricultural commissioner, Reed Rexford, said in 1965 that, "The prime concern will be to find ways to allow small farmers to continue operating even if they get out of milk production." Diversification of farm products and exploration of farmland for recreational use were two possibilities.

- Governor Deane Davis created the Commission that developed Act 250, prioritizing the protection of prime and statewide soils and criteria for land development.

- Governor Thomas Salmon recommended the result of a Seal of Quality for agricultural products meeting high standards, the development of consumer food cooperatives, farmers markets, and more direct farm sales and food processing facilities, and work toward reducing dependence on outside food sources.

- Governor Richard Snelling supported the farm sector programs including the Current Use Forestry and Agricultural Taxation Program, and legislation to bar the sale of detergents that would increase algae growth.

- Governor Madeleine Kunin created a Commission on Vermont's Future: Guidelines for Development. The Commission pointed out that, "Agriculture is not only of economic importance, but it is also the source of much of our character, strong work ethic, sense of independence, fix it and make it work."

- Governor Dean supported the Dairy Compact and the purchase of development rights.

- Governor Jim Douglas supported the dairy industry with state funding during a pricing crisis in early 2000 and other activities, including acquiring development rights, methane digesters, energy efficiency on farms, and greater farm diversification.[284]

The above is only a partial list of 20th century Vermont governors and their activities relating to the agriculture of the state and productive land use. It is intended to show that many governors have been challenged to address the loss of farms in the state and address the competition that exists in markets over a long period. The support of the state's delegation in Washington during these years was of further assistance in sustaining land use and agriculture in the state.[285] Vermont has maintained delegation membership on the U.S. Senate Committee on Agriculture, which continues today.

Marketing Vermont

A Seal of Quality Program for Vermont-made agricultural and food products was created in 1982 to increase consumer awareness of the quality and value of Vermont agriculture and food products. Other states in the region had developed efforts around branding, for example "Jersey Fresh for New Jersey." As Secretary of Vermont Agriculture in 2010, I suspended the Vermont Seal of Quality, as the Agency needed more funding and staffing to ensure the standards were followed. Following that decision, extensive work was done with many around the 400-year celebration of Lake Champlain to envisage terroir or geographic indicators like D.O.C. for place-based foods similar to France and, on a smaller scale, in Quebec.[286]

An article by Stephanie Shapiro in the *Baltimore Sun* on June 15, 2008 mentioned the value and appeal of the Vermont brand: "Since the mid-1980s, when a handful of Vermont products were first featured at a New York City Fancy Foods Show, the former republic has become its distinctive brand in a fashion true to its self-reliant nature."

Twenty years ago, with support from then-Govenor Madeleine Kunin and a marketing visionary named Jerome Kelley, Vermont first promoted its natural essence in bottles of maple syrup, jars of jam, and pâté. The state became a model for similar efforts around the nation.

"We were sort of the first out of the gate in marketing a product from a region that has this cachet," says Jennifer Grahovac, a Vermont Agency of Agriculture marketing specialist. "When you put Vermont on a product, it means something to consumers." A Seal or Brand was recognized as an essential way to differentiate Vermont products of unique value in the market and the state.

Vermont specialty products continue to receive recognition in the regional and national markets. And while the State of Vermont no longer uses a Seal of Quality or another distinguishing image or quality standard on products produced, many individual marketing efforts to do so have been successful.

An Activist Era
for the Environment

IT WAS 1969, AND THE CUYAHOGA RIVER WAS BURNING. The fire—and the man-made conditions that caused it—caught national attention in *Time*, *National Geographic*, and other publications. The shock and call to action that resulted produced the creation and passage of the Federal Water Pollution Control Act of 1972.[287]

There had been federal action relative to water before the 1972 Water Pollution Control Act (for example, the 1899 Rivers and Harbors Act and the 1948 Water Pollution Control Act) that provided federal loans for wastewater treatment plant construction and grants for state and local agencies to investigate pollution sources. However, it was only the 1972 Act that mandated an active approach with states to address water quality by applying water quality standards to interstate waters and state waters, encompassing all surface waters in the country.

The 1972 law enshrined several key provisions, including the Section 208 Planning process with the states; Section 318 management plans to address non-point source pollution; and Section 303(d) TMDL, or Total Maximum Daily Load for water quality. Section 404 gave the U.S. Army Corps of Engineers jurisdiction over all navigable rivers. Relative to non-point pollution from farms in Vermont, the program was to be managed by the State Agency of Agriculture, Food, and Markets. Farmer Watershed Groups such as the Champlain Valley Farmer Coalition, the

Connecticut River Watershed Farmers Alliance, and the Franklin and Grand Isle Farmer's Watershed Alliance were organized to help address the issues relating to farming and water quality.

Other Federal key environmental policies of the time include:

- Wild and Scenic Rivers Act of 1968

- Conservation as a prerequisite for participation in USDA programs, sodbuster and swamp buster, the Conservation Reserve Program (CRP), and the 1985 Farm Bill.

- Clean Air Act of 1970

- National Environmental Policy Act 1970

- Federal Clean Water Act of 1972 (referred to as Clean Water Act)

- Endangered Species Act of 1973

- Safe Drinking Water Act 1974

The Food Security Act of 1985 is considered the turning point in agricultural conservation policy in the United States, with the shift in focus from agricultural resource conservation management to environmental management with sodbuster and swamp buster provisions. Also, until the 1996 Farm Bill was enacted, no conservation programs dealt explicitly with animal waste management issues, EQIP, or Environmental Quality Incentive Program.

Vermont's Act 250

Vermont leaders had already begun to take action to protect the environment before the flurry of federal activity in the late '60s and early '70s. With the Interstate Highway System, Vermont became much closer to Boston and New York City, and with the promotion of tourism it became the "Beckoning Country." Southern Vermont towns became major skiing destinations built on environmentally sensitive mountainsides. Governor Deane Davis, a native Vermonter and a Republican, was concerned that the state had virtually no environmental safeguards.[288] In creating the Gibb Commission, Chaired by State Representative Arthur Gibb in

1969, Governor Davis recognized the need for more controls and wanted their administration to be at the local or district level in the state.[289] The Commission held well-attended hearings around the state before recommending to the legislature a new statewide regulatory system for reviewing and controlling plans for large-scale and environmentally impactful development. This recommendation is what is widely known today as Act 250 in Vermont.

Early environmental protest

Governor Davis insisted that the new regulatory system not be centered in Montpelier—that the power of review of projects and grant permits be vested more locally, in a group of regional commissions. This led to the creation of District Environmental Commissions, of which membership is comprised of laypersons, not government officials. A modest professional staff supports these commissions in reviewing the ten criteria of the Act.

Act 250 made a legal process for reviewing and controlling large-scale and environmentally impactful development plans in sensitive areas. Protecting or mitigating prime and statewide agricultural soils has been a critical part of the process. Act 250's Criterion 9(B) Primary Agricultural Soils recognizes that soils of "prime," "statewide," and "local" importance are valuable natural resources to Vermont and its residents. The regulatory review process for a proposed development assesses whether the outcome may reduce the land's agricultural potential. In cases where sensitive farmland is at risk, two methods provide for mitigating the loss of agricultural potential: onsite mitigation and offsite mitigation.

In an interview with the Associated Press in 1998, on his 90th birthday, Arthur Gibb said that, "Act 250 had played a crucial role in saving what makes Vermont special." He went on to say that "it leads to responsible development, and when you think of the irresponsible development we had in 1969 . . . Thank God for Act 250."

Pesticide Controls and Tension Around Environmental Regulation

Silent Spring by Rachel Carson awakened the world to the effects of pesticides on the natural world[290] when it was published in 1962. According to one article, although the chemical industry attacked the work as anti-science and anti-progress, Carson was known to believe that chemicals had their place in agriculture. "She favored a restrained use of pesticides, not a complete elimination, and did not oppose judicious use of manufactured fertilizers," writes Harvard University sustainability scholar Robert Paarlberg. This view happened to put her at odds with the fledgling organic movement. Since her book *Silent Spring,* there has been increased global and U.S. concern over pesticide usage and their implications for environmental sustainability and human health. Scientists also are increasingly interested in understanding how pesticide exposure affects honey bee colonies and pollination as these colonies have declined in Europe and North America.

In 1972, the US EPA granted Vermont approval to enforce its pesticide control program. In 2022, the Vermont Agency of Agriculture proposed amending pesticide rules for the first time in 31 years. To this day, the Vermont Agency of Agriculture, Food, and Markets posts Vermont Pesticide Usage Summaries in the state.

Once introduced to North America in the mid-1800s, commercial fertilizers were increasingly used to help bring fertility back to depleted soils. As a result, and due to concern over the quality of products sold, the state in 1882 passed a law authorizing fertilizer sales but required a license from the State of Vermont to sell them. UVM was permitted by state law to test the samples. It was reported at the time that, "One of the greatest wastes in Vermont was over-fertilization."

Today the sale of fertilizers is licensed by the Agency of Agriculture. The program provides for registering, inspecting, and analyzing all commercial fertilizer products sold in the state. Likewise, each brand of graded lime must be registered before being sold in the state.

The Vermont Agency of Agriculture is responsible for managing and enforcing the Required Agricultural Practices (RAPs), the standards to which all farms are held to reduce the impact of agricultural activities on water quality. The RAPs include required practices and management strategies, some of which apply to all farms and others of which are specific to certain sizes of operations or environmental factors.

The historic Act 250 in 1970 established key land development and environmental stewardship procedures with preference given to statewide and prime soils for agricultural production. Other laws address the state's resource issues as well. Over the years Vermont has developed a regulatory approach within agriculture that has established rules for medium and large farm operations and their nutrient management plans. "Vermont law provides that persons engaged in farming and following accepted agricultural practices as described by the Secretary of Agriculture by rule shall be presumed to comply with water quality standards." There are two kinds of enforceable standards: 1) farmers must follow Accepted Agriculture Practices, and 2) the Secretary of Agriculture may require best management practices on a case-by-case basis. The law requires that standards be enforceable and cost-effective.

Vermont works closely with other state agencies, the University, USDA, NRCS, and FSA on cooperative approaches to the issues, including the Lake Champlain Basin Program (a collaborative approach to water quality and resource issues between Vermont, New York, and the Province of Quebec), and farmer and citizen watershed organizations. Nevertheless, the pollution of streams and lakes due to human activity, including farming, remains politically charged and volatile.

Climate change is also having an impact on land use and farming in Vermont. As the climate shifts, some areas may become less suitable for agriculture, promoting changes in land use. Farmers may choose to diversify their operations and some land may be repurposed for conservation or other uses. These impacts highlight the need for Vermont farmers and policymakers to adopt resilient agricultural practices and to develop strategies to mitigate the effect of climate change on farming and land use. Restoration of ecosystems and conservation efforts will also be critical in maintaining agricultural productivity in the face of these challenges.

Use Value Appraisal Tax Appraisal

A law passed in 1978 created the Current Use Tax Program for agriculture and forest land. The legislature and Administration recognized the need to tax farm and forest land on its use rather than its development potential.[291] Currently, more than 19,000 parcels totaling more than 2.5 million acres of land are enrolled, about one-third of Vermont's total land. Once the property has been registered, it will continue in the program unless it is withdrawn by the owner or by Property Valuation Review; if it is converted or developed, it becomes ineligible. If the landowner changes or creates the land use, the landowner may be assessed a Land Use Change Tax. The Division of Property Valuation and Review program is administered within the Department of Taxes. For forestry land under the program, a ten-year management plan must be submitted to the County Forester.

Vermont Housing and Conservation Board

The pace and pattern of development in Vermont in the mid-1980s threatened the rural character of the state and settlement patterns. A coalition of concerned organizations and interests came together in 1987 to pass the Vermont Housing and Conservation Trust Fund Act.[292] The primary goals of this Act were to ensure affordable housing and conserving and protecting Vermont's agricultural land, forestland, historic properties, critical natural areas, and recreational lands from privatization and development. The work is often done in collaboration with others, including the Vermont Land Trust, established as a private not-for-profit in 1977 to protect farmland, forestland, and community lands within the state. Under the program, a conservation agency or land trust purchases the development rights from the landowner and legally protects the land from development. The landowner may continue to use the land for designated purposes such as farming and recreation. Almost all PDR programs are funded by tax revenues and tax-deductible donations. According to the report, "Purchase of Development Rights (PDR) Programs: Have We Paid Too Much?" by Dr. Qingbin Wang and graduate student Brian Silver of UVM's Department of Community Development and Applied Economics in 2000, the Vermont Housing and Conservation Board has spent about 29 million dollars to purchase the development rights of approximately 70,000 areas of land since the inception of the state's PDR program in 1987.[293]

Unique State Agricultural Lending Programs
Vermont Economic Development Authority (VEDA)

VEDA was created in 1974 with one of its goals to assist farmers in restructuring their balance sheets.[294] A cyclical downturn in the dairy industry had negatively impacted farmers financially and the Vermont Agricultural Credit Corporation (VACC) was formed within VEDA in 1999 to focus more on the business of farms and farming and their financial needs in the state.

Since 1999, agricultural lending through VACC has grown to 40% of VEDA's direct loan portfolio. Initially more than 90% dairy, VACC's portfolio is becoming more diversified as the Vermont agricultural economy expands to include new farm operations. According to agricultural lending data from VEDA, the agricultural portfolio has grown from $8.5 million in 1999 to just over $100 million at the beginning of 2021. While dairy at one time accounted for the largest concentration of the portfolio, it has been declining with increased diversification in the agricultural and forestry sectors. Dairy Cattle and Milk Production, as of 2021, still accounted for 61 percent of the loans; some of this lending is done with USDA Farm Service Agency guarantees as well.

CHAPTER TEN

A Renaissance of the Past

I N HIS 1938 BOOK *Speaking from Vermont*, Governor George Aiken wrote that, "Agriculture today is no longer principally a matter of producing crops. Perhaps we can say that the greatest problem of agriculture today is keeping up with the times and adapting itself to the challenges which come to it in rapid succession."[295]

Overview of Post-WWII Changes in Technology on the Farm

Great farm production leaps occurred in the U.S. after World War II. Bayer Global, writing in "How Has Technology Changed Farming?" lists many of the strides that have accelerated production over the last 60 years. The list includes:

- The Green Revolution of the 1960s and the work of Dr. Norman Borlaug to develop a growing process that allowed plants to thrive with new irrigation and crop management techniques;

- The development and use of glyphosate or Roundup® herbicides by farmers to control weeds in their products (subject to increased scrutiny and investigation);

- Development of rotary combines in 1975 that cut and separated crops in one pass over the field;

- The first genetically modified plant cell by Monsanto Company in 1982; genetically modified crops are engineered for resistance to insects, viruses, and drought among other crop protection solutions;

- Satellite technology advances that allow farms to see their operations from overhead to drive large equipment, better track their fields' performance, and plan based upon data;

- In the 2000s, software and mobile devices became available to assist farmers to have better harvests. Today there are drones, robots, and "intelligent" tractor technologies that help farmers reach new levels of precision and efficiency in crop management;

- Digital platforms in 2010 began to combine data from on-farm practices and agronomic models with local weather and soil conditions to provide better management information. At the same time, precision breeding began delivering crops with improved yields and more resilience;

- In 2012, CRISPR technology opened the door to genome editing to design seeds with increasingly desirable characteristics such as improved yield or quality profiles, resistance to diseases and pests, and even climate resilience;

- In the 2020s, A.I., machine learning, and digital modeling are being used to revolutionize agriculture by analyzing and interpreting ever larger and more diverse sets of data in new ways.

Understanding the Past Reinforces the Future

History may not repeat itself, but it can often come close, it is sometimes said. In many respects, a review of history alongside what is taking place today reveals what I would call a "Renaissance of the Past." The renewed interest in agriculture and local food systems within our state is both heartening and exciting.

The Renaissance that I see manifests itself in many forms, including the growth of community-supported agriculture (CSAs), farmers' markets, food hubs, new products, and new farmers, the further diversification of agriculture production with various products from the land and animals that are raised on the ground—all accompanied by the continuous evolution of agricultural technology. This rebirth or Renaissance further reinforces the connections across Vermont's past, present, and future.

It has been said that "if agriculture were to wither away to memory, Vermont would cease to be anything unique. It would become just a distant suburb of Boston, its character defined by tourist restaurants and shopping malls. Not only does living agriculture contribute so much to the character of Vermont, but it is also indispensable to preserving the landscape, which in our time has become a vital component of the state's economic attractions."[296] Others have made similar conclusions: "Defined by its iconic rural countryside of farms, forests, villages, and small cities, Vermont's working landscape has emerged as key to the brand and quality of life of the state and its future. In many ways, the land shapes Vermont's culture and identity; perhaps this is at the root of Vermont's perceived authenticity and attractiveness to visitors from around the world."[297]

A 2008 forum of dairy leaders on the dairy industry at the Windham Foundation's Grafton Conference, "Seeking to Ensure the Future Viability of Vermont's Dairy Industry," addressed ways to help better sustain dairy farming. (At the time, there were about 1100 dairy farms in the state versus around 500 today).[298] The forum found that "Vermont is losing national influence as the number of dairy farms, allied businesses, and milk production decline. Commodity milk production is increasingly concentrated in intensive large dairy herds in the south and West of the Country, where production costs are lower. This is compounded by an aging population of dairy farmers and many dairy farms that need modernization but need to be capitalized."

Vermont's strengths continue to be the relatively large consumer population close by, the attractiveness of the Vermont brand which makes its products more attractive, the strong tradition and culture of dairy farming, and the growing entrepreneurship of the sector. Many believe that a competitive future for Vermont dairying increasingly depends on local manufacture of high-quality dairy products that aren't made anywhere else, and building and capitalizing on the status of the Vermont brand.

How the Past Has Helped to Define the Future

Vermont maple production

Vermont's agriculture, forests, and working landscape have always defined the state. It has always been a state of constant change. The early settlers who came to Vermont from Southern New England after the French and Indian War looked for productive soil and new opportunities. They followed the Abenaki, who had used many places for food production and fishing.[299] While the early settlers were subsistence farmers, planting a few crops and keeping a few animals for their use, increasingly, many began raising items for sale or barter as towns and nearby cities grew. They found grain, potatoes, and livestock markets in Montreal, Quebec, Troy, Albany, and Boston. In the early 1800s, significant cash-crop exports included potash, pearlash, whiskey, pork, beef, wheat, flour, grain, butter, cheese, lumber, and horses. In the Champlain Valley before 1820, growing grains was a significant agricultural enterprise, and those grains were either distilled locally or hauled to markets in Albany or Troy.

Maple syrup gradient

Apple collection

Land and water transportation were integral in developing industry and trade in agriculture and other products. Road building began in the late 1700s with private turnpikes chartered by the state legislature. Canal and water transportation became as crucial as overland routes. In Bellows Falls, on the Connecticut River, the first canal built in the U.S. began in 1792. This canal allowed our state's producers to ship several tons of products to Hartford, Connecticut on flat-bottomed boats in just 3 days.

Burlington became a flourishing center of commerce on the west side of the state after completion of the 64-mile Champlain Canal in 1823. The access provided by these transportation networks to new markets grew increasingly crucial to the economic health of Vermont farms as the farm economy evolved from subsistence and barter to a cash basis. These new transportation networks also exposed products from the state to new competition farther afield. Railroads proved to be a mixed blessing to Vermont farmers who witnessed dire economic realities as competition from Western wool, beef, butter, and grain forced changes in the farm economy.

As agriculture changed in response to market conditions and competition, specialization grew and farmers focused on specialty crops, livestock, and livestock products. In the early 1800s, when disease, pests, and increased competition undermined grain production in the Champlain Valley, many farmers adapted by raising Merino sheep. The grass was "king" in the hills and valleys of Vermont, which proved ideal for these sheep. Many towns had flocks of one thousand or more, and

Vermont became known as the sheep capital of the world, home to over one and a half million head. These sheep were envied for their fine wool and fleece and were in great demand worldwide. Nevertheless, Vermont and its Merino sheep fell captive to tariff regulations, international events, and competition from the Western U.S. and abroad.

While this specialization was taking place, other products continued to be produced. The 1850 agricultural statistics illustrate product diversification: butter, cheese, oats, beef, wheat, barley, rye, buckwheat, field beans, potatoes, hay, orchard products, flax, hops, hemp, silk, maple sugar, maple syrup, honey, and wool.[300]

Vermont had already established itself as an essential maple-producing state, which was also valid for its apple production. Many farms produced maple syrup in the spring, providing important income diversity. Orchard farming began as early as the 1810s on Isle La Motte. Large-scale orchards were established along Lake Champlain in the late 1800s and in other parts of Vermont later.[301] Vermont shipped its maple and fruit products throughout the U.S. and abroad, enhancing Vermont's agricultural diversity and notoriety.

Following the Merino sheep industry's decline, there was a slow migration to the specialization in butter and cheese production. These products were traditionally made on the farm, with skills passed down from generation to generation. As cities and towns grew, merchants reached out for these products and demand outstripped production capacity and the uneven quality of on-farm production, leading to the development of creameries and cheese factories. St. Albans had the world's largest commercial creamery and Vermont butter soon became known for its quality; products from the state even won a gold medal for the best butter in the world. As demand for Vermont's dairy products grew, creameries sprang up in many towns and communities around the state. By 1904, 186 creameries and 66 cheese factories operated throughout Vermont.[302] Whole industries supported this production, including cheese and butter box production and specialty churns. This changed as cities further south reached out for fluid milk, and the first milk train left Bellows Falls, Vermont, for Boston in 1890.

Haying in Vermont

Commercialization of dairying and the interstate shipment of milk and milk products created renewed economic challenges, and farmer cooperatives became important in bargaining for fair pricing for their members with supportive federal laws like Capper-Volstead. Federal actions relative to dairy price supports and parity pricing could not forestall the pressure for change and the eventual beginning of the deregulation of the dairy industry in the early 1980s. Early farm leaders, many of whom had witnessed these changes in Vermont agriculture over time (loss of Merino sheep, butter markets, grain production, beef trade) and had been part of it, recognized the competitive advantages of farming in Vermont. A critical advantage was being near emerging markets in the Northeast and growing and producing products of the highest quality to meet changing consumer needs.[303] Others saw the benefit of growing grass and raising animals that could convert grass to energy. Many agreed that Vermont farmers could never compete with the West on a commodity-pricing basis.

Through the years, farmers have had to adapt to changes. Today, consumers have renewed interest in local and regional foods. Vermont farmers are taking the lead in many areas, including being known for organic dairying and other healthy, locally produced food products. This renewed interest in local foods has resulted in growing farmers' markets, food hubs, CSAs or community-supported agriculture, farmstead cheese production, farm-raised beef, new maple products and production, new vineyards, pick-your-own fruit operations, breweries, and many other products from the farm. Maple is still considered the soul, and dairy anchors Vermont agriculture.

Vermont today is increasingly known for its food systems, an authentic connection to the land, and the strength of the Vermont brand. This brand manifests itself in the working landscape, a clean environment, a place of recreation and tourism, quaint villages, scenic vistas, notable cheeses, local foods and beverages, and friendly and hospitable citizens. This Vermont brand helps to support and define our state, its past, present, and future. It helps support a vibrant tourist industry and connects people to places. In 2009, *National Geographic Traveler* rated Vermont as the number five place in the world.[304] It is a true Renaissance, reinforced by the many products produced on or from the land.

The Foundation of Vermont Agriculture and the Future

The continuing trend in the loss or closing of dairy farms remains familiar in Vermont and throughout New England.[305] As far back as the late 1930s, George Aiken and others proposed the consolidation of the Vermont dairy industry for specialization in high-grade products, such as butter and cheese. Governor Aiken's proposal advocated reconsidering the Vermont go-it-alone policy of specialized dairy manufacturing, which Commissioner Brigham had sponsored in the post-World War I period.[306] In a Vermont milk report, "the two men envisioned that Vermont might become the Denmark of the United States, noted for its quality butter, cheese, and milk-fed bacon."[307] Aiken and his predecessor as governor, Charles Smith, finally advocated Vermont becoming part of the federal milk market order in the 1937 Agricultural Adjustment Act, as there was no alternative at the time. It remains that way today.

This direction, emphasizing specialty product production and marketing, was introduced previously. Others had advocated the need for high-quality products in the market.[308] Other governors and their administrations also recommended new ways or different approaches to sustain a viable working landscape as marketing challenges from products produced further West came into the markets served by Vermont farmers. Diversification of the farm with many products was seen as one way to avoid economic strife.

The Vermont Brand gained value in the market early. It has been awarded in many ways in the past, for example. The Merino Sheep won awards in Europe, as did Vermont-produced butter, which continues with farm-produced cheeses and other products, including beer. Vermont was known for many specialty kinds of cheese and other food products. This value was further embellished with many national and international awards.[309] Other value products have come to the market and helped establish Vermont as a food or specialty product location in the public's mind, like the beer trails,[310] cheese trails,[311] Community Supported Agriculture, and other specialty product locations to include wine, spirits, roadside stands, and farmers markets. Even a Locavore Index was created to help measure this impact.[312]

What Is the Future for Vermont Farms and Food Systems?

Today, challenges on the farm continue. To take stock and identify a new path forward, the Vermont Sustainable Jobs Fund, authorized by the Vermont legislature in 2019, created the "Vermont Agriculture and Food System Strategic Plan for 2012-2030."

The plan identified 15 strategic goals with 87 objectives and 34 priority strategies. In a bid to secure collective buy-in and overwhelming support, the report was shaped by farmers, food entrepreneurs and workers, government personnel and elected officials, nonprofit organizations, technical and business assistance providers, educators, researchers, capital providers, and Vermont food consumers. In all, over 1,500 people from all of these groups contributed to the development of this plan over 18 months. The state has used the Working Landscape funding initiative[313] and other financial resources to increase sustainable dairy farming in the state.[314] More recently, Governor Phil Scott followed the trend of many of his predecessors in addressing significant investments in agriculture.[315]

Local farm

The joint work of the Vermont Department of Agriculture and the Vermont Council of Humanities, in eight public forums around the state, raised the question, "Does Farming or Forestry Have a Future in Vermont?"[316] This was also a period of economic change and pricing challenges. Many felt the future was product diversification on the farm and smaller-scale agriculture. One noted County Agent in Bennington County said, "farming in the future will be the source of subliminal income rather than complete self-reliance on the farm for payment, and the further that goes in that direction, the better." Even at the University of Vermont, the well-known state extension agronomist at that time, Win Way, supported that trend toward smaller farms. "He traced the emphasis from grain to sheep to cows and said cows may not be the final answer. He said he saw the future as small, highly diversified, part-time operations."

Small-scale farming requires support and incubation. It is encouraging to see that happening in the state with people of all backgrounds farming today.

Local dairy cows

Farm production

Today on the Land

The trends on the farm and with the land appear more urgent today but are not new either.[317] A paper on that subject in 2018 outlined the risks and challenges well.[318] It found in its review "that the agricultural landscape, and the people who work that land, are essential to Vermont's communities, economy, and culture. However, these resources are at risk. We anticipate that a combination of unfortunate market forces and a generational transfer of assets will transform our agricultural sector in the next decade in many ways that Vermonters will not like; the crisis is most visible in the state's conventional dairy industry, though vegetable and livestock farmers and organic dairy producers are also facing significant market-based challenges. Nearly all farming sectors are confronted with downward price pressure on producers, increasing production expenses, a need for increased marketing and sales savvy to sell products in an increasingly competitive and complex marketplace, challenges in transitioning assets to a new generation of owners, and an ongoing shift in our economy and cultural traditions away from land-based agriculture towards processed foods." They noted that the agricultural economy had diversified widely over the past two decades, and the industry has a more entrepreneurial spirit. Many young individuals are interested in diversified, rather than dairy, farming in our state and region. But despite this innovation and diversification, the resulting agricultural activity is not happening at the scale necessary to utilize the best acreage that is leaving dairy operations. Some of Vermont's more profitable farm business models utilize less farmland than the traditional dairy farm model.

Common Themes of the Past for Farm and Food Systems

While the issues relative to farm viability and the working landscape are more visible and urgent today, they are not new based on a review of the past. As others have said, "our past manifests our ideals, but they also beckon us to the future." In that respect, this book is not intended to predict the future or any course of action that should be taken to help better sustain a working landscape. It has, however, uncovered some common themes about the past that may help guide the future.

Many hard-working families and various organizations are dedicated to these tasks. The book and the chapters that have captured or reviewed the rich history are intended to help identify those things that have helped create a more sustainable food system and working landscape. These are:

- Not to compete with the West on a commodity basis and to develop those products that consumers in the nearby markets will need. Vermont farmers can compete on a different production scale than large Western farms and should utilize technology and innovations to lower costs and increase efficiency in marketing their products.[319] Ways to enter, sustain, or maintain markets are essential. However, it isn't easy to penetrate markets today without significant capital for operations, even within cooperatives.[320] This has been seen over the years within the cooperatives operating in Vermont and more recently with St. Albans Cooperative in their merger in 2019 with Dairy Farmers of America, the largest dairy cooperative in the U.S. Today there is no dairy cooperative with their headquarters in the state. And there should be.

- Diversification of products produced on the farm, from various types of farms, and in the community is essential, helping to avoid economic strife and supporting local and family food needs. Specialization and reliance on one product from the farm increases financial risks, especially in the production scale needed to compete in the commodity market and consolidated grocery retail trade today.

- Vermont, like many other states, faces challenges in finding domestic workers willing to engage in agricultural jobs, which often require long hours and hard physical labor. Guest workers can fill these gaps, ensuring that farms operate efficiently. The availability of guest workers will also depend on immigration policies and programs, which can change over time. Ongoing advocacy for fair and accessible programs for agricultural workers will be crucial in maintaining this workforce.

- Mixed sources of funding support at the state, federal, and local levels and from private sources will continue to be necessary for maintaining a working landscape and productive and financially sustainable farms. This has become more challenging as most of the population nationally, and elected officials, are disconnected from the farm, whereas they were quite connected in the distant past. Bold new strategies are needed as have been identified to include payment for ecosystem services and those services that working farms provide in keeping the landscape open.

- Soil, water, and environmental health are essential and something that Vermont must continue to take leadership in doing and promoting. A movement toward the lowest ecological impact possible with farm operations is necessary for maintaining and building public support. As the climate shifts, some areas may become less suitable for agriculture, prompting changes in land use. Farmers may choose to diversify their operations, and some lands may be repurposed for conservation or other uses. Education on suitable practices and funding for adaptation initiatives will play a vital role. As the climate changes, the types of crops that can be successfully grown may shift to those crops that can withstand the stresses of a changing climate. Climate change is having significant impacts on both the ski industry and maple syrup production as well.

- Collaboration (terroir and quality standards) and cooperation and coordination around marketing, production, and processing are essential for better pricing and efficiencies for all-size farm operations. Overall, cooperation and collaboration among farmers and food makers and organizations in Vermont and the region contribute to a more robust food system that enhances resilience, promotes sustainability, and fosters greater community support. This is important for the health and growth of the agricultural sector.

- Research, teaching, and extension education are critical for all aspects of farming, including land use, new product development, promotion, and climate change strategies. The "three-legged stool" of Research, Teaching, and Extension Education was created not just to deal with the status quo but to help determine and help guide Vermont farms and food systems into the future.[321]

- The landscape is essential for farms that need access to suitable productive land and for promoting tourism. The two are crucial connections recognized as far back as the late 1800s. Increased fragmentation of the best farmland is possible as farms leave dairy farming, and new strategies are needed to maintain this valuable productive resource base.[322]

- Local foods and spirits of all types help to further Vermont's rich history of a state embedded with the past but understood to be necessary to its future that helps to connect people with the land and those that produce products from the ground.[323]

- Consumers are not connected to the farm today as they were in the distant past. This requires increasing efforts to help the public understand how the food they consume is produced. It also means that farmers cannot take the public's understanding or support for granted. Coalitions and other means to reach nonfarmers are increasingly and critically necessary.

- Farming and local foods are essential to Vermont's tourism strategy creating a unique and authentic experience that encourages visitors to engage with local culture, history, and the natural environment. Promoting these elements not only boosts the tourism industry but also supports local farmers and contributes to the state's economy.

With all the background and past and current work of many organizations in developing actions for the future, even the development of a plan to pay for ecosystem services to farmers for their contribution to the environment, economy, tourism, and landscape is complicated as it requires transformative changes, new sources of capital, as well as technological, pragmatic and market development that does not currently exist.[324] However, there are few good options without bold new approaches of this kind. "Our concern for the future will guarantee our future," but it will continue to take new thinking and renewed action to do so. Each generation and each administration within the state, working with the state legislature and federal congressional delegation, has espoused the importance of farming and the working landscape, and that continues. Despite many programs and studies over the years, Vermont agriculture continues to be at a crossroads. Vermont's agricultural and food systems are influenced by global trends and local realities. A focus on sustainability, resilience, community engagement, and technological innovation will be key to navigating future challenges and opportunities. The future of Vermont farming is set to evolve significantly in response to climate change, local food demand, land use, tourism, federal and state policies, and various farming models. The interplay of these factors will shape a dynamic and evolving agricultural landscape in Vermont.

Over many years, Vermont has developed programs at many levels within the state for sustaining farms, often in collaboration with federal partners. It will continue to take enlightened leadership both on the farm and within the policy arena to advocate for the agricultural sector and the working landscape. The challenges will be many and they will continue as they have over the past. As the late Governor George Aiken said in 1938, "The greatest problem of agriculture . . . is keeping up with the times and adapting itself to the changes which come in rapid succession." Overall, the future of farming in Vermont will depend on the ability of farmers, policymakers, and communities to navigate these challenges and opportunities while maintaining the state's agricultural heritage. This book is dedicated to all of those who continue to do so.

Afterword

THIS BOOK IS INSPIRED BY MY UPBRINGING on a small hilltop farm in rural Southern Vermont, as well as my professional experiences afterward. Throughout my journey, I have been fortunate to learn from many individuals, including family, friends, colleagues, farmers, and various leaders inside and outside of government.

At the University of Vermont, I studied the economics of agriculture and dairy farming. As a young U.S. Army officer stationed in West Germany, I observed effective land management practices and recognized the importance of local farmers' markets. My role as a Sea Grant Specialist with Cornell University taught me about supply management in commercial fisheries and the significance of coastal zone and land use management.

Upon returning to Vermont, I became the first manager of the state's 208 nonpoint source agricultural project. I later served as a consultant for the governor's Current Use Value Taxation Program for farmland and forestry. Subsequently, I joined Congressman Jim Jeffords's team as a staff member on the U.S. House Agriculture Committee, where I contributed to the passage of the first national agricultural land protection bill as part of the 1982 Farm Bill.

Despite our efforts, we were unable to establish a supply management program for the U.S. conventional dairy industry. However, history shows that such a program was essential for a more stable dairy farming sector in Vermont and the surrounding region. I also played a role in the passage of the 1985 and 1987 Farm Credit Acts while working at the Springfield Farm Credit Banks and Bank for Farmer Cooperatives. Afterward, I co-founded an international trade company with a colleague that developed export markets for U.S. value-added products in emerging European markets. I also worked on a global market development team for a law firm in Washington, D.C.

In addition, I served as Chair of the Animal and Animal Products International Trade Advisory Committee to the U.S. Secretary of Agriculture and the U.S. Trade Ambassador. I participated as a non-governmental organization representative during the Seattle Round of Multilateral Trade Negotiations. These experiences provided me with valuable insights into international agricultural trade and U.S. and international trade policies.

Eventually, I returned to Vermont and was appointed Executive Director of the USDA Farm Service Agency for the state, overseeing programs that supported Vermont farm operations. Later, I served as Vermont's Secretary of Agriculture and subsequently as a senior advisor to the President of Vermont Technical College. My last professional responsibility was as the CEO of Grace Cottage Hospital and Health Care in Townshend, Vermont, where I learned about the importance of rural and community health and local food systems connected to better health.

My personal and professional journey has provided me with a comprehensive understanding of farm and food policies and programs at local, national, and international levels. My love for Vermont, its land, the people who work it, and our local communities—historically reliant on an agricultural economy—stems from this background. I am grateful for my upbringing and the experiences I have encountered. I hope my professional work has positively impacted others as well as the farm and rural communities along the way.

Acknowledgements

I OWE THE COMPLETION OF THIS BOOK to the unwavering support of my wife, Ann. I also want to acknowledge the encouragement from many others who inspired me to write this book on Vermont's agricultural history, drawing from my own experiences and passion for the state's agricultural heritage.

I extend special thanks to those who financially supported the Center for the Study of Vermont at the University of Vermont for this publication. These individuals include Orly Munzing and the former Board of the Strolling of the Heifers in Brattleboro, who highlighted the dairy industry and agriculture in Vermont through their programs; Crea Lintilhac of the Lintilhac Foundation, renowned for advocating the responsible use and management of natural resources in pursuit of a more robust and healthier Vermont; and Angelo Pizzagalli, who emphasized the need for action to address the economics of the dairy industry during my tenure as Vermont Agricultural Secretary and continues to uphold that commitment to Vermont agriculture.

I also want to honor the late Will Rapp, a pioneer in Vermont's socially and ecologically responsible business community and an advocate for environmental stewardship, as well as Judy and Carl Farenbach, who established the High Meadows Fund to support practical and innovative environmental and societal solutions.

I am grateful for the support from others who recognized the importance of understanding how the past influences the future. The publication of this book faced numerous delays due to management and staffing changes at the Center at UVM. I appreciate those who stepped in to help, including Richard Watts, who dedicated himself and the staff to its publication; Trisha Denton, former Coordinator of the Center for Rural Studies at UVM who committed her time and resources and talents to the completion of this book; and Lars Hasselblad, a volunteer editor. I also want to acknowledge the UVM CRS student interns who assisted with pictures and illustrations, particularly Katherine Mcgee.

Finally, I would like to thank Linda Roghaar and the staff at White River Press for bringing the book to its final publication. Since this book is a publication of UVM and the Center for the Study of Vermont, I hope it achieves its goal of helping people understand how past changes influence the future of agriculture and farming in the state, and how farmers and their families continue to adapt to challenges while working the land with attention to environmental stewardship.

Endnotes

1   Sarah Hoyt Brown Park and Hazel Park Potter, *The Park Family in America*, Library of Congress CS71.P235 1964

2   Walter Hill Crockett, "Vermont The Green Mountain State," Volume One, (The Century History Company, Inc., 1921), page 259

3   Roger Allbee, "Sustainable Agriculture in the State of Vermont: The Roots and Branches of an Enduring Relationship," in *The Vermont Difference, Perspectives from the Green Mountain State*, Ed. by J. Kevin Graffagnino, H. Nicholas Muller III, David A. Donath, Kristin Peterson-Ishaq, Woodstock Foundation and Vermont Historical Society, 2014

4   "Celebrating Intervale History: The Land" in https://www.intervale.org

5   Crockett, Volume Two, page 508

6   Ibid, page 209

7   Townshend Historical Society, *A Stitch in Time*, 2003, page 29

8   Dorothy Canfield Fisher, *Vermont Tradition: The Biography of an Outlook on Life*, (Boston: Little, Brown and Co.), 1953

9   Charles Stickney, "The local history of Brookline, Vt: The general history of the town," at https://archive.org

10 *Annals of Brattleboro, 1681–1895*, Compiled and Edited by Mary R. Cabot, Volume 1, Press of E. L. Hildreth & Co., 1921, page 217

11 The Dummerston Historical Society, "Dummerston, An 'Equivalent Lands' Town 1753–1986," ed. by Alice Crosby Loomis and Frances Walker Manix, Book Crafters, Chelsea Michigan, page 127

12 Crockett, Volume 1, page 266

13 Fisher, page 182

14 Ibid, page 183

15 Mike Sutton, "A revolutionary casualty," at https://www.chemistryworld

16 David Ciceri, A. C. Manning, and Antoine Allanore, "Historical and technical developments of potassium," at https://dspace.mit.edu

17   Walter Crockett, *History of Vermont*, Volume 2, pages 509–512

18   Charles Stickney, *The Local History of Brookline, Vermont*

19   Crockett, Vol. 3, page 177

20   Crockett, Vol. 2, page 511

21   *Rural Vermont: A Program for the Future*, The Vermont Commission on Country Life, Burlington, 1931, page 61

22   Jacqueline B. Car, "Local History and the Vermont Borderlands, 1790–1820," in *Vermont History* 84, no. 1 (Winter/Spring 2016), pages 70–92

23   Ibid, page 70-92

24   Charles Stickney, "The Local History of Brookline, Vermont"

25   "West Brattleboro/Molly Stark Byway—The Historical Marker," www.hmdb.org

26   "The History of the Poultney Turnpike," The Poultney Historical Society

27   Ibid

28   Ibid

29   Ibid

30   Crockett, *History of Vermont*, Vol. 2, page 521

31   H. Nicholas Muller III, "Jay's Treaty: The Transformation of Lake Champlain Commerce," in *Vermont History* 84, no. 1 (Winter/Spring 2016): 70–92

32   Ibid

33   Ibid

34   Ibid

35   Bellows Falls Canal, Vermont Historical Society, Vermonthistory.org

36   "River Flat Boat, Connecticut River," Rockingham Library Historical Society, www.rockinghamlibrary.org

37   John Holbrook, "An Industrial Era," Chapter XXII, *Annals of Brattleboro, 1681–1895*, by Mary R. Cabot, Vol. 1, Brattleboro, Vermont, E. L. Hildreth & Co., 1921

38   *Life on a Canal Boat, The Journals of Theodore D. Bartley, 1861–1889*, edited by Russell P. Bellico, for the Lake Champlain Maritime Museum, by the Purple Mountain Press, Fleischmann's, New York, 2004

39   Car, "Local History and the Vermont Borderlands"

40   "A Little Short of Madness: A Brief History of the Erie Canal," in www.eriecanal.org

41   Dr. Ann Green, Univ of Pa, Presentation to the Wilton Ct. Historical Society on Feb 23, 2014, on Lake Erie and its impact on commerce

42   Melancthon W. Jacobus, "A Canal Across Vermont," *Vermont History* XXIII, no. 4, (October 1955), vermonthistory.org

43   Mark Bushnell, "Then Again: Vermont catches 'canal fever'," *VTDigger*, June 2, 2019, vtdigger.org

44   "Historical Context: The Railroads and New York's Canals," Consider the Source *New York*, considerthesourceny.org. In an effort to protect its canals, the New York

legislature forbade the railroad, but only during winter months. Then in 1844, state lawmakers permitted freight on the railroad, but only during the winter months.

45   "The Sheep That Shaped New England," Today in Connecticut History, April 10, 2020, todayincthistory.com/2020/04/10/april-10-david-humphreys-brings-the-sheep-that-shaped-new-england/

46   "David Humphreys, Soldier, Statesman, and Agricultural Innovator," in Connecticut History, August 26, 2021, connecticuthistory.org/david-humphreys/

47   Mary Pepperell Sparhawk Cutts, "The Life and Times of Honorable William Jarvis of Weatherfield," Nabu Press, 2010

48   "The Spanish Sheep Craze That Forever Changed Vermont," New England Historic Society, newenglandhistoricalsociety.com

49   Ibid

50   History of Town of Weathersfield, Vermont

51   Robert F. Balivet, "The Vermont Sheep Industry: 1811–1880," Vermont Historical Society, *Vermont History* XXXIII, no. 1 (January 1965)

52   Miriam Chapin, "Sheep in Vermont," *Vermont Life* XIII, no. 3 (Spring 1959)

53   Denise Williams, "Merino Mania: A Nineteenth-Century Fiber Craze," *Spinoff*, January 2, 2023, spinoffmagazine.com

54   *History of Vermont*, Vol. 3, page 195

55   *History of Vermont*, Vol. 3, page 196, and *Nile's Register* of July 23, 1825, on the tariff and its impact on the stability of the sheep industry in Vermont

56   Chapin, "Sheep in Vermont"

57   Betty Jane Belanus, "They Lit Their Cigars With Five Dollar Bills: The History of the Merino Sheep Industry in Addison County"

58   Ibid

59   "The Spanish Sheep Craze That Forever Changed Vermont," New England Historical Society

60   "Exhibition at Hamburg," *Report of the Commissioner of Agriculture for the Year 1863*, Government Printing Office, Washington, D.C., 1863

61   Ibid

62   Anthony F. Hall, "Elkanah Watson, George Perkins Marsh and the Making of the Adirondack Landscape," *Lake George Mirror*, November 30, 2020

63   Ibid

64   Crocket, *History of Vermont*, Vol. 3, page 391

65   Lynn A. Bonfield and Mary C. Morrison, *Roxana's Children, The Biography of a Nineteenth-Century Vermont Family*, University of Massachusetts Press, 1995

66   Mark Busnell, "Then Again: Youthful exodus from Vermont actually began in the early 1800's," *VTDigger*, March 28, 2021, vtdigger.org

67   Crocket, *History of Vermont*, Vol. 3, page 270

68   Paul Heller, "The Great Silkworm Excitement in the Green Mountains," *The Times Argus*, Sept. 2, 2019

69   Mark Bushnell, "Then Again: Fairbanks brothers built St. Johnsbury's economy," *VTDigger*, Oct. 1, 2017, vtdigger.org

70   Mark Bushnell, "Then Again: On and off the prohibition wagon," *VTDigger*, Feb. 19, 2017, vtdigger.org

71   *Rural Vermont: A Program for the Future*, The Vermont Commission on Country Life, 1931

72   Corin Hirsch, "Resurrecting Hops, Vermont brewers watch and wait as local growers try to create an industry," Seven Days, August 3, 2011, www.sevendaysvt.com

73   Steven R. Hoffbeck, "'Remember the Poor' (Galatians 2:10): Poor Farms in Vermont," *Vermont History* 57, no. 4 (Fall 1989).

74   Dr. R. R. Sherman, of St. Albans "Origin of the St. Albans Butter Market," A Paper Read Before The Vermont Board of Agriculture, At Its Meeting At St. Albans, March 6 and 7, 1872, *First Annual Report of the Vermont State Board of Agriculture, Manufactures and Mining For The Year 1872*, Montpelier, J. & J. M. Poland's Team Printing Establishment, 1872, pages 158–165

75   Denise A. Raymo, "All Aboard the Butter Train," *Press-Republican*, September 12, 2010

76   R. R. Sherman, "Origin of the St. Albans Butter Market," page 164

77   Ibid, page 161

78   C. W. Mudgett, of Weathersfield, "Associated Dairying," in *Third Biennial Report of The Vermont State Board of Agriculture, Manufactures and Mining for The Years 1875–76*, by Henry M. Seely, Secretary to the Board, Tuttle & Co., Rutland, 1876, page 81

79   D. B. Wheelock, Esq. of Barre, "The Butter Dairy," An Essay Read by the Meeting of the State Board of Agriculture, in the *First Annual Report of the Vermont State Board of Agriculture, Manufactures, and Mining for the Year 1872*, page 143

80   C. Horace Hubrard, of Springfield, Vt., Agricultural Editor of the Vermont Record and Farmer, "Vermont Cattle," A Paper Prepared For The Meeting Of The Vermont Board Of Agriculture, at Newport, August, 1872, In *First Annual Report of the Vermont State Board of Agriculture, Manufacturing, and Mining for the Year 1872*, pages 293–306

81   L. S. Hardin, "Making Butter," in *Fourth Report of The Vermont Board of Agriculture for The Year 1877*, by Henry M. Seely, Secretary of The Board, J. & J. M. Poland's, Montpelier, 1877, pages 101-104

82   Wheelock, "The Butter Dairy," page 153

83   *Records of the Vermont Dairymen's Association*, ArchiveGrid, researchworks.oclc.org

84   "Billings Farm Timeline," Billings Farm & Museum, at billingsfarm.org

85   George Aitken, "Breeding, Care and Management of Dairy Stock, Etc.," Presentation to Vermont Dairymen's Association, *Twentieth Annual Report of the Vermont State Board of Agriculture, for the Year Ending June 30th, 1900*, Opinion Publishing Co, Bradford, 1900, page 72

86   H. W. Vail of North Pomfret, "Butter and Butter-Making," *Tenth Vermont Agricultural Report by The State Board of Agriculture for The Years 1887–1888*, by W.W. Cooke, Secretary of The Board, Free Press Association, Burlington, 1888, page 25

87   War & History: Holy Cow in Vermont History, Freedom and Unity, Vermont Historical Society

88   Ibid

89   Ibid

90   "Dairying, Bennington Institute, Vermont Agriculture Report," *Eleventh Vermont Agriculture Report by the State Board of Agriculture for the Years 1889–90*, Argus and Patriot Book and Job Printing House, Montpelier, Vt. 1890, page 47

91   Osgood was on the Board of Directors of the Newfane Creamery. My late grandmother's diary says that one day my grandfather "carried cream to the creamery and got a check for $27.32."

92   Wheelock, "The Butter Dairy," page 143

93   Victor I. Spear, "VERMONT, A Glimpse of Its Scenery and Industry," *Thirteenth and Fourteenth Vermont Agricultural Report Issued by The State Board of Agriculture for the Years 1893 and 1894*, by C. M. Winslow, Secretary to the Board, Free Press Association, Burlington, 1894, pages 275-279

94   Sherman, "Origin of the St. Albans Butter Market," page 163

95   Amanda Thiubaut, "This Place in History: Montgomery Mills," Vermont Historical Society, February 13, 2020

96   The Vermont Farm Machinery Company, fullersteamdivision.com 2019/01/30

97   Ibid

98   G. S. Fassett, of Enosburg, "Needs of The Dairy," *Fifth Report of The Vermont Board of Agriculture for The Year 1878*, by Henry M. Seely, Secretary of The Board, J. & J. M. Poland's, Montpelier, 1878, pages 55–63

99   G. F. Wright, of Bakersfield, "The Vermont Farmer's Future," A Paper Read at A Meeting of The State Board of Agriculture, at St. Albans, March 6th and 7th, 1872, in the *First Annual Report of The Vermont State Board of Agriculture, 1872*, pages 510–524

100 G. G. Small, of Morrisville, "Butter Making in Competition with The West," *Second Biennial Report of The State Board of Agriculture, Manufactures and Mining, 1873–74*, pages 120-128

101 M. O. Howe, "The Merits of our State," Fiftieth Public Meeting held at Fayetteville, Tuesday and Wednesday, February 1st and 2nd, 1876, *State Board of Agriculture Report of 1875–1876*

102 Lyman W. Peet of Cornwall, Vt, "Eastern and Western Farming," Read before the Institute at Middlebury, in *Eighth Vermont Agriculture Report by The State Board of Agriculture, 1883–84*, pages 187–191

103 *Tenth Report of the State Board of Agriculture, 1888–1889*

104 *15th and 16th Report of the State Board of Agriculture, 1894–1895*

105 Rollin C. Smith, of Pittsford, Member of the Board, "What Crops Should Vermont Farmers Raise," *Tenth Vermont Agriculture Report, 1887–1888*, pages 338-342

106 "The Future of the Vermont Farmer," *Rutland Herald and Globe*, 1879

107 Kathy Padden, "Napoleon and The Invention of Margarine," Today I Found Out, todayifoundout.com

108 "Crimes Against Butter: The Oleomargarine Controversy," April 12, 2022, newyorkalmanack.com

109 "Fat Change: The War Between Butter and Margarine," Neatorama, April 7, 2014, neatorama.com

110 Jesse Rhodes, "Food Dye Origins: When Margarine Was Pink," *Smithsonian Magazine*, April 7, 2011

111 G. W. Simpson, of Boston, in an address to Fourteenth annual winter meeting of the Vermont Dairymen's Association in Burlington, in the *Eighth Vermont Agricultural Report by The State Board of Agriculture for the Years 1883–1884*, by Hiram A. Cutting, M.D., Ph.D., Secretary of The Board, Watchman & Journal Press, Montpelier, 1884, page 81

112 "Oleomargarine," Remarks of William W. Grout of Vermont, in the House of Representatives, May 25, 1886, on the bill to tax oleomargarine. Government Printing Office, Washington, D.C., 1886, Internet Archive, https://archive.org/details/oleomargarine00grou/page/n1/mode/2up

113 "The Butter vs. Margarine Wars Sweep Vermont in 1900," New England Historical Society, newenglandhistoricalsociety.com

114 "After surpassing butter in the 1950s, Americans' per capita consumption of margarine is now below that of butter," USDA ERS-Chart Detail, July 18, 2016. see https://www.ers.usda.gov/data-products/chart-gallery/

115 *Margarine Wars*, www.fandango.com

116 See ERS Chart Detail above

117 Donald A. Frederick, "Antitrust Status of Farmer Cooperatives: The Story of the Capper-Volstead Act," *U.S. Department of Agriculture, Cooperative Report 59*, September 2002, page 6

118 Ibid

119 Ibid, page 7

120 Andrea Rebek, "The Selling of Vermont: From Agriculture to Tourism, 1860–1910," *Vermont History* 44, no. 1, (Winter 1976), Vermont Historical Society

121 Manufacturing and Mining for the Years 1873–1874, 2nd Annual Report of the State Board of Agriculture, Manufacturing, page 275

122 Seth M. Zoracki, "Vermont's Tradition of Education and The Vermont Constitution," *Albany Law Review*, Vol. 69, 2006

123 Erin Judge, "The Middlefield Fair: A Case Study of The Agricultural Fair in New England (Nineteenth Century)," seniors honor project in history, Westfield State University, December 2016

124 William Brewer, "Agricultural Societies: What They Are and What They Have Done," *Connecticut Agriculture Annual Report, 1880-1886*

125 "Vermont County Fairs, 1924," *Vermont History*, Vermont Historical Society

126 "American Traditions: A Short History of Agricultural Fairs," Yesterday's America, yesterdaysamerica.com

127 Chris Burns, "Negotiating Community Values: The Franklin County Agricultural Society Premium Lists, 1844–1899," University of Vermont ScholarWorks, scholarworks.uvm.edu

128 "United States Agricultural Society," Wikipedia, en.wikipedia.org

129 "Frederick Holbrook," Wikipedia, en.wikipedia.org

130 Nathan M. Sorber, *Land-Grant Colleges and Popular Revolt: The Origins of the Morrill Act and the Reform of Higher Education*, Cornell University Press, 2018

131 "Smithson to Smithsonian The Birth of an Institution," Smithsonian Institution Archives

132 "Jonathan Baldwin Turner: Reformer and Visionary," Illinois History & Lincoln Collections, publish.illinois.edu/ihlc-blog/2018/09/14

133 National education—system of. Memorial of Alden Partridge..., www.loc.gov .resource.serials 26th Congress 2d Session, Doc. no. 69, House of Representatives, January 21, 1841.

134 "Memorial Addresses on the Life and Character of Justin S. Morrill, February 22, 1899, delivered in the Senate and House of Representatives, Fifty-Fifth Congress, Third Session," Government Printing Office, Washington, D.C. 1899.

135 William Belmont Parker, *The Life and Public Services of Justin Smith Morrill*, (Boston: Houghton Mifflin Co., 1924)

136 "Justin Smith Morrill," www.encyclopedia.com, June 11, 2018

137 "Lincoln Signs the Morrill Land Grant Act of 1862," in WikiSummaries, November 10, 2022

138 Parker, *Justin Smith Morrill*

139 "Lincoln Signs the Morrill Land Grant Act of 1862," in WikiSummaries, November 10, 2022

140 "Pacific Railroad Acts," Wikipedia, en.wikipedia.org

141 The Central Pacific Co. and the Union Pacific Co. were the two chosen to construct this massive railroad across the U.S. One from the Pacific coast, and the other from the East. They met in Promontory Point, Utah on May 10, 1859, changing the face of the U.S. and its agricultural system.

142 "The U.S. Land-Grant University System: Overview and Role in Agricultural Research," *Congressional Research Service Report R45897*, Updated August 9, 2022, https://crsreports.congress.gov

143 Edwin C. Rozwenc, "Agricultural Education In Vermont," *Vermont History* XXVI no. 2, April 1958. This article by Rozwenc has a very in-depth history of Morrill's role in the Land Grant Act and actions within the State of Vermont in accepting the provisions of the act to include the attempt to merge UVM, Middlebury, and Norwich into one Land Grant Institution in the State of Vermont.

144 Robert Lee and Tristan Ahtone, "Land-grab universities," *High Country News*, March 30, 2020, hcn.org

145 Guy B. Horton and Henry A. Stoddard, *The Grange in Vermont,* (St. Johnsbury, Vt.: The Cowles Press, 1968)

146 "The Grange Movement, 1875," The Gilder Lehrman Institute of American History, www.gilderlehrman.org

147 "The Winslow Compromise," *Vermont History* XXXI, no. 2, April 1958

148 James Mascarene Hubbard, "Education in Vermont," *The Atlantic*, July 1914

149 *First Annual Report of the State Agricultural Experiment Station*, State of Vermont, The Tuttle Co, Official State Printers, Rutland, 1888

150 Robert D. Daniels, "The University of Vermont: The First Two Hundred Years," and Robert Sinclair "Agricultural Education and Extension in Vermont," University of Vermont, 1991

151 Alfred Charles True, *A History of Agricultural Education in the United States, 1785–1925*, Government Printing Office, Washington, D.C., 1929

152 *Rural Vermont: A Program for the Future,* The Vermont Commission on Country Life, Burlington, Vt., 1931, page 103

153 www.census.gov

154 *Rural Vermont: A Program for the Future,* The Vermont Commission on Country Life, Burlington, Vt., 1931, page 10

155 Ibid, The People of Vermont, pages 10-33

156 *2nd Annual Report of the State Board of Agriculture, Manufacturing, and Mining for the Years 1873-1874*, page 275

157 Paul Searls, "Major Valentine's Swedes," *Vermont History* 81, no. 2 (Summer/Fall 2013), pages 139-169

158 Ibid

159 "Used Vermont Farms, Things Said and Done," *Rutland Herald*, Nov. 23, 1904

160 Paul Searls, "Major Valentine's Swedes," *Vermont History* 81, no. 2 (Summer/Fall 2013), pages 139-169

161 Ibid

162 Paul Searls, *Repeopling Vermont: The Paradox of Development in the Twentieth Century,* (Vermont Historical Society, 2019), page 79.

163 Andrea Rebek, "The Selling of Vermont: From Agriculture to Tourism, 1860–1910." *Vermont History* (Winter, 1976):14-27

164 *Twenty-Fourth Annual Report, State Board of Agriculture for the year ending June 30, 1904*, by C. J. Bell, Secretary, Press of the Economist Co., Troy, N.Y., 1904, page 23

165 *Report of the Country Life Commission, 60th Congress, 2d Session, Senate Document no. 705*

166 Theodore Roosevelt Center, Dickinson State University

167 E. S. Brigham, St. Albans, "The Outlook for Vermont Farming," in Agriculture of Vermont, *First Annual Report of the Commissioner of Agriculture of the State of Vermont, 1909*, Capital City Press, Montpelier, pages 155-161

168 "Address by the President of the Vermont Dairymen's Association," *Twenty-Eighth Annual Report, State Board of Agriculture 1908*, page 32

169 Charles Otis Gill and Gifford Pinchot, *The Country Church, The Decline of Its Influence and The Remedy,* Published Under Authority of the Federal Council of the Churches of Christ in America, The Macmillan Co., New York, 1913

170 *Agricultural Cooperation and Rural Credit in Europe.* American and U.S. Commissions, 1913. Senate Doc. no. 214, Parts 1, 11, In 63rd Congress.

171 "Farm Bureau Notes," "Cooperative Societies," in *News and Citizen* (Morrisville, Vt.), Apr. 16, 1924

172 Charles Otis Gill and Gifford Pinchot, *Six Thousand Country Churches,* Macmillan Co., New York, 1919

173 Charles Otis Gill's history and life can be found at wikipedia.org. In his retirement in 1929, he relocated to Waterford, Vt where he took up farming until his death in 1929. Gifford Pinchot is noted as one of the leading conservationists and first chief of the U.S. Forest Service.

174 In 1900, there were about 240 independent creameries in Vermont, including 30 cheese factories. In 1915, 60 to 75 percent of the creameries in Vermont were owned by the few large milk dealers of the Boston milkshed. See Edwin Charles Rozwenc, *Agricultural Policies in Vermont, 1860-1945,* Vermont Historical Society, 1981, page 143

175 Ibid, page 139

176 "The Rustic's Viewpoint," *Brattleboro Reformer,* Wednesday, April 16, 1930. It discusses the closing of the Wardsboro, Vt. creamery after Newfane and Wilmington and the new competition with Brattleboro and Bellows Falls.

177 James I. Stewart, "The Economics of American Farm Unrest, 1865–1900," Economic History Association, February 10, 2008, EH.net/encyclopedia /the-economics-of-american-farm-unrest-1865-1900/

178 "Interstate Commerce Act (1887)," National Archives, www.archives.gov

179 Donald A. Frederick, "Antitrust Status of Farmer Cooperatives: The Story of the Capper-Volstead Act," *Cooperative Information Report 59, Rural Business Cooperative Service,* USDA, September 2002

180 Percy W. Bidwell, "The Agricultural Revolution in New England," *The American Historical Review* 26, no. 4 (July 1921), pages 683–702

181 *First Annual Report of the Vermont Commissioner of Agriculture, 1909,* Capital City Press, Montpelier, Vermont

182 "History of UVM Extension," The University of Vermont, https://www.uvm.edu .extension

183 E. S. Brigham, St. Albans, "The Outlook for Vermont Farming," *Agriculture of Vermont, First Annual Report of the Commissioner of Agriculture of the State of Vermont, 1909,* Capital City Press, Montpelier, pages 155–161

184 *Agriculture of Vermont, Fifth Annual Report of the Commissioner of Agriculture of the State of Vermont, 1913,* St. Albans Messenger Co., pages 12–13

185 *Agriculture of Vermont, Sixth Annual Report of the Commissioner of Agriculture of the State of Vermont, 1914,* St. Albans Messenger Co., page 16

186 Edwin Charles Rozwenc, *Agricultural Policies in Vermont, 1860–1945,* Vermont Historical Society, 1981, pages 143–146

187 James L. Guth, "Herbert Hoover, the U.S. Food Administration, and the Dairy Industry, 1917-1918," *Business History Review* LV, no. 2 (Summer 1981), also published online by Cambridge University Press: 11 June 2012

188 R. M. Washburn, *Agriculture of Vermont, Second Annual Report of the Commissioner of Agriculture of the State of Vermont 1910,* The Capital City Press, Montpelier, 1910, pages 64–67

189 Rochdale Principles,Wikipedia.org

190 Lynn Pitman, "History of Cooperatives in the United States: An Overview," revised December 2018, UW Center for Cooperatives, University of Wisconsin–Madison, resources.uwcc.wisc.edu/History_of_Cooperatives.pdf

191 Woodsmoke Productions and Vermont Historical Society, "The Co-op Movement, 1919,"The Green Mountain Chronicles radio broadcast and background information, original broadcast 1988-89, https://vermonthistory.org/the-coop-movement-1919

192 Thomas Bradlee, "The Farm Bureau of Today," *Agriculture of Vermont, Tenth Report of the Commissioner of Agriculture State of Vermont, for the biennial period, July 1, 1918 to June 30, 1920,* pages 59–65

193 In the beginning the Farm Bureau and Extension were joint organizations. In Vermont, the county Farm Bureau received Extension funds. On November 24, 1954, USDA Secretary Benson of the Eisenhower Administration issued a memorandum effectively severing the tie between the Extension Service and Farm Bureau. Shortly after, the state extension services and Farm Bureau severed their ties. See "Celebrating 100 Years of the American Farm Bureau Federation—Part 1 (10/11/2019)," The Friday Footnote, footnote.wordpress.ncsu.edu.2019

194 Donald A. Frederick, "Antitrust Status of Farmer Cooperatives," page 92

195 *Tenth Report of the Commissioner of Agriculture for the State of Vermont, Thirty-Fourth Annual Report of the Vermont Maple Sugar Makers' Association,* page 9

196 "Report of Dairy Manufacturing Specialist, V. R. Jones," *Agriculture of Vermont, Eleventh Biennial Report of the Commissioner of Agriculture for the State of Vermont, 1920–1922,* St. Albans Messenger, 1922, page 31

197 Ibid, pages 35–43, "Report of L. G. Mulholland, Field Agent in Marketing"

198 Ibid, page 37

199 *Thirty-Fourth Annual Report of the Vermont Sugar Makers' Association,* in *Agriculture of Vermont, Fourteenth Biennial Report of the Commissioner of Agriculture of the State of Vermont, 1926–1928,* pages 15-16

200 "The History of Eastern States," *Eastern States Cooperative Farmers Handbook,* 1950, Eastern States Farmers' Exchange, Inc., West Springfield, Ma.

201 Frances M. Gagnon, *Eastern States Exposition, An Illustrated History at 75 Years,* Eastern States Exposition, Springfield, Ma

202 Each State has a building on the grounds of Eastern States Exposition, referred to as the Big E today. Vermont's building was built in 1929 on land that belongs to the State of Vermont. Each year agricultural and other products from Vermont are marketed at the Vermont Building during the Big E. The building during that time is managed by the State Agency of Agriculture.

203 George D. Aiken, *Speaking from Vermont,* Frederick A. Stokes Co., New York, 1938, pages 45–61

204 L. A. Cooley, "Marketing Vermont Products," *Twenty-Second Annual Report of the Vermont Horticultural Society, Fourteenth Annual Report of the Commissioner of Agriculture, 1926–1928*, pages 17–19

205 *Agriculture of Vermont, Eighth Annual Report of the Commissioner of Agriculture, 1916*, page 19

206 "President's Address," *Thirtieth Annual Report of the Vermont Maple Sugar Makers' Association, Twelfth Biennial Report, Commissioner of Agriculture of the State of Vermont, 1922–1924*, St. Albans Messenger Co., 1924, page 4

207 In her diary, my late grandmother Ruth Osgood Allbee writes about daily life on the Allbee farm in Brookline in the early 1900s and how diversified it was then with pigs, chickens, maple, cows and cream shipped to the creamery. "Big garden's and changing. Making brine to cure the hams from the pigs. Sawdust for the ice house. Caring for the sheep. Sugaring in the spring. Churned butter. Went to the grist mill."

208 "Victory Gardens in World War I," The National WWI Museum and Memorial, Vermont History, theworldwar.org/learn/about-wwi/victory-gardens-world-war-i

209 "World War I: Camp Vail, 1916," Vermont History, vermonthistory.org/world-war-i-camp-vail-1916

210 Brian C. Albrecht, "The WWI Agricultural Boom and Bust," American Institute for Economic Research, November 15, 2018, aier.org/article/the-wwi-agriculture-boom-and-bust

211 Mary Zell Galen, "When the Federal Government Washed Away Mutual Aid: Response to the Great Vermont Flood of 1927," Office of Student Research, Longwood Senior Theses, Longwood University, 2019

212 Arthur Stone, *The Vermont of Today*, "Chapter XI, The Great Flood of 1927," Lewis Historical Publishing Co., Inc., 1927

213 Juliane B. Eastmann, *Historical sketch of the Granite City Cooperative Creamery Association, Inc., Barre, Vermont*, Jan 1, 1940, located at the Vermont Historical Society library in Barre

214 *Rural Vermont: A Program for the Future*, The Vermont Commission on Country Life, Burlington, 1931, page 2

215 Chris Graff, *Dateline Vermont*, "No. 3: The Flood of Vermont," Thistle Hill Publications, North Pomfret, Vt., pages 217–218

216 *Rural Vermont: A Program for the Future*

217 "1932 United States Presidential election in Vermont," Wikipedia

218 "Creating An Image: The Government Lends A Hand—Freedom & Unity," Vermont History, vermonthistory.org/freedom-unity-government-lends-a-hand

219 Jeff Potash, Gene Sessions, and Michael Sherman, "Vermont in the Great Depression, 1929," *Vermont History*, Vermont Historical Society

220 Ibid

221 "Personal Report of the Commissioner of Agriculture E. H. Jones," *Agriculture of Vermont, Sixteenth Biennial Report of the Commissioner of the State of Vermont, 1930–1932*

222 Robert Daniels, editor, *The University of Vermont: The First Two Hundred Years*, University of Vermont, 1991

223 Dr. Don Paarlberg, "Tarnished Gold: Fifty Years of New Deal Farm Programs," *Imprimis*, November 1987, Vol. 15, Issue 11

224 Theodore Saloutous, *The American Farmer and The New Deal*, The Henry A. Wallace Series, The Iowa State University Press, Ames Iowa, 1982, page 16

225 Dr. Don Paarlberg, "Effects of New Deal Farm Programs on the Agricultural Agenda a Half Century Later and Prospect for the Future," *American Journal of Agricultural Economics* 65, no. 5, Oxford University Press, Dec. 1983, pages 1163–1167

226 James H. Shideler, "Herbert Hoover and the Federal Farm Board Project, 1921–1925," *The Mississippi Valley Historical Review* 42, no. 4 (Mar 1956), pp 710–729

227 Henry Morgenthau, Jewish Virtual Library

228 "Henry A. Wallace (1933–1940)," UVA Miller Center, millercenter.org

229 Clifford B. Gregory, "The American Farm Bureau Federation and the AAA," *The Annals of the American Academy of Political and Social Science* 179, pages 152–157

230 Douglas Bowers, Wayne D. Rasmussen, and Gladys L. Baker, "History of Agricultural Price-Support and Adjustment Programs, 1933–84," *Agricultural Information Bulletin no. (AIB-485)*, USDA Economic Research Service, 1984

231 *The Barre Daily Times*, January 10, 1936

232 Don Paarlberg, "Tarnished Gold: Fifty Years of New Deal Programs," *Imprimis* 16, Issue 11, November 1987. Everyone, even many ag economists and others in the policy environment were not pleased with the New Deal programs and what they were meant to achieve.

233 "Federal Control of Milk Advocated," *Lewiston Maine Daily Sun*, June 26, 1937

234 "Opinion: Milk Price Regulation Protects Consumers," *The New York Times*, October 8, 1994

235 "The Boston Milk Case," *Lewiston Maine Daily Sun*, May 5, 1936

236 "Farewell address of George D. Aiken as it appears in the Journal of the Joint Assembly for 1941," Vermont Secretary of State, sos.vermont.gov

237 *Rural Vermont: A Program for the Future*, Vermont Commission on Country Life, 1931, page 79

238 Calvin Covington, "Federal Milk Marketing Orders: History, Purpose, and Future," *Dairy Industry News*, Progressive Dairy, Feb. 28, 2013, agproud.com

239 Henry Morgenthau, Jewish Virtual Library

240 George D. Aiken, *Speaking from Vermont*, Frederick A. Stokes Co., New York, 1937, page 50.

241 "Dust Bowl," HISTORY, www.history.com/topic/great-depression/dust-bowl

242 Timothy Egan, *The Worst of Times, The Untold Story of Those Who Survived the Dust Bowl*, Houghton Mifflin Co., 2006

243 "Roosevelt Urges States to Create Conservation Districts," www.riceswcd.org, May 8, 2017

244 "Resettlement Administration (RA)," encyclopedia.com

245 Sara M. Gregg, "Can We 'Trust Uncle Sam'? Vermont and the Submarginal Lands Project, 1934–1936," *Vermont History*, Vermont Historical Society

246 *The Barre Times*, 24 September 1936

247 Vermont Commission on Country Life 1931, pages 147–148

248 Karen R. Twitchell, "Agricultural Stabilization and Conservation Service: History, Policy and Problems," *So. Dakota Law Review*, 31 S.D.L. Rev. 425, 1986, also at nationalaglawcenter.org

249 Mark Bushnell, "Then Again: A 1930s plan had Vermont paving its peaks," *VTDigger*, August 5, 2018, vtdigger.org

250 Vermont Commission on Country Life 1931, page 131

251 Ibid, page 131

252 Peter S. Jennison, *Roadside History of Vermont*, page 249

253 Hannah Silverstein, "No Parking: Vermont Rejects Green Mountain Parkway," *Vermont History* 63, no. 3 (Summer 1992), Vermont Historical Society

254 For an interesting commentary on the proposed Parkway, read an article by Historian Bruce Post, "The national park that got away" in *The Burlington Free Press*, March 4, 2016

255 My wife's grandfather, the late Dr. Ernest Bancroft of So. Barre, Vermont was a proponent of the Parkway, and he organized the Friends of the Green Mountain Parkway arguing that it was the only opportunity for a greater degree of prosperity in the state. Bancroft, a noted veterinarian at the time, was the CEO of the Barre City Cooperative Creamery and a noted dairy leader who was a member of the Vermont Commission of Country Life.

256 Wayne D. Rasmussen, "New Deal Agricultural Policies after Fifty Years," *Minnesota Law Review* 68, scholarship.law.umn.edu/mlr/2489

257 *Rutland Herald*, "Agriculture," Monday Morning, April 15, 1940, page 8

258 Arthur Woolf, "The impact of Interstate highways 89 and 91 on Vermont's economy and demographics," benningtonmuseum.org/library/walloomsack/volume-10/the -impact-of-interstate-highways-89-and-91-on-vermonts-economic-development .pdf

259 Ibid

260 *Rural Vermont: A Program for the Future*, The Vermont Commission on Country Life, page 129, says in one recommendation on Summer Residents, "as rapidly as possible, the state should extend the scope of the Vermont State Bureau of Publicity, which has been of large service to our people since it was first established nearly twenty years ago. Money spent wisely in advertising and developing Vermont should be considered an investment rather than an expenditure."

261 Kevin Ellis, "The Beckoning Country," www.kevinkellis.com

262 Graff, *Dateline Vermont*, page 216

263 Clifford Cameron, *Farms, Flatlanders, and Fords: A Story of People and Place in Rural Vermont, 1890–2010*, West Hartford, Vt, 2011

264 Dr. Fred Webster, "Memories of Local Delivery of Milk," *Rutland Herald*, November 11, 1996

265 Monument Farms Dairy, www.monumentfarms.com

266 Austin Danforth, "Iconic Vermont milk producer Thomas Dairy to close at the end of September," *Burlington Free Press*, September 11, 2020

267 "History: Local milk production changes with economies of scale," by The Brattleboro Historical Society, *Brattleboro Reformer*, June 24, 2022; also see "The Day the Milkman Went Away: A History of Home Milk Delivery," www.drinkmilkinglassbottles.com

268 "The Traditional History of the Milkman," The Better Milk, April 22, 2021, www.thebettermilk.com

269 Arthur Neal, "How One Man's Invention Changed Food Access World-Wide," Technology, usda.gov/media/blog /2012/02/21/how-one-mans-invention-changed -food-access-world-wide

270 Dr. Fred Webster, "Memories of Local Delivery of Milk," *Rutland Herald*, November 11, 1996

271 "Wallace Gives Views on Milk Tank Situation," *Bellows Falls Times*, Thursday April 22, 1954

272 Mark Bushell, "Then Again: Bulk milk tanks altered the family farm way of living," *VTDigger*, Jan 13, 2009, vtdigger.org

273 Editorial, "Vermont Hilltops Losing Importance," *The Newport Daily Express*, Sept. 20, 1955, page 2

274 Howard Ball, "From 'One Town, One (or Two) Vote(s)' to 'One Person, One Vote': The Impact of Reapportionment on Vermont, 1777–1992," *The Proceedings of the Vermont Historical Society* 61, no. 2 (Spring 1993)

275 Kevin McCallim, "Vermont's Last Dairy Farmer-Lawmaker Is Selling His Cows," *Seven Days*, February 5, 2020, sevendaysvt.com

276 Graff, *Dateline Vermont*, page 217

277 "Freedom & Unity: Modern Vermont 1950–Today," Vermont History, Vermont Historical Society, vermonthistory.org/freedom-unity-modern-vermont

278 Dan Chodorkoff, Jake Guest, Roz Payne, Roger Fox, Grace Gershuny, Jim Higgins, Liz Guest, Larry Kupferman, "Colleges, Communes & Co-ops in the 1970s: Their Contribution to Vermont's Organic Food Movement: Excerpts from the 175th Annual Meeting of the Vermont Historical Society, September 21, 2013," *Vermont History* 82, no. 2 (Summer/Fall 2014)

279 "Dorothy Thompson's Vermont Journal: Thompson's Land Corps," Vermont Public Radio, in American Archive of Public Broadcasting, also see Mark Bushnell, "Then Again: Dorothy Thompson's army of farm volunteers," *VTDigger*, May 17, 2020

280 Ibid

281 "'Plowing Old Ground' Exhibit Puts Focus on Vermont's Organic Farming Pioneers," The Cornucopia Institute, Last Updated June 17, 2013

282 Kate Daloz, *We Are As Gods, Back to the Land in the 1970s on the Quest for a New America*, PublicAffairs, New York, 2016

283 Overview of Act 250, legislature.vermont.gov, Jan 16, 2019, also at Vermont Natural Resources Board, History of Act 250, nrb.gov

284 Vermont Jobs Fund and Vt Agency of Agriculture and Food Systems Strategic Plan: 2021–2031 Strategic Plan for Vt Agriculture and Food System at www.vtfarmtoplate.com

285 In 1979 U.S. Congressman Jim Jeffords (R-VT) hired me as his staff person in the U.S. House Committee on Agriculture of which he was a member. One of his priorities which we passed as part of the 1982 Farm Bill (with the support of Rep. Tom Foley (D-WA) the Chairman of the House Committee on Agriculture, and Senator Patrick Leahy (D-Vt) was the first national agricultural land protection act. We also attempted to pass a national milk supply and demand control program to bring about stability in dairy pricing at the time that the old parity pricing was too high and resulted in too much milk being produced at a huge cost to the federal government. A supply control system was rejected by the then leader of the National Milk Producers Federation, the lobbying arm of dairy cooperatives. As a result, the deregulation of the dairy industry continued after but with various attempts to bring better pricing with the whole herd buyout, dairy termination program, the federal dairy compact initiative, and various initiatives since that time. The loss of dairy farms in Vermont continues due to an unstable federal pricing system that was established in 1938.

286 Vermont Agency of Agriculture, Food & Markets, Researching Taste of Place in Vermont, December 2010, Center for Rural Studies, University of Vermont

287 Jennifer Latson, "The Burning River That Sparked a Revolution," TIME, June 22, 2015, time.com

288 "The Origins of Act 250: A Talk With Former Governor Deane C. Davis," *Vermont Environmental Report*, Fall 1989

289 Overview of Act 250, legislature.vermont.gov, Jan 16, 2019, also at Vermont Natural Resources Board, History of Act 250, nrb.gov

290 Jennifer Weeks, "'Silent Spring' 60 years on: 4 essential reads on pesticides and the environment," The Conversation, October 11, 2022, theconversation.com

291 "Current Use and Value Appraisal Program," Agency of Agriculture, Food and Markets, agriculture.vermont.gov. Also see "About the Program," Vermont Department of Taxes, tax.vermont.gov

292 "Mission & History," Vermont Housing & Conservation Board, www.bhcb.org. Also see "About Us—Vermont Land Trust—Our farms, our forests, our future," vlt.org

293 Qingbin Wang and Brian Silver, "Purchase of Development Rights (PDR) Programs: Have We Paid Too Much?" American Agricultural Economics Association Annual Meeting, July 30–August 2, 2000, Tampa, Florida

294 About the Vermont Economic Development Authority (VEDA), www.veda.org /about-veda/

295 George D. Aiken, *Speaking From Vermont*, Frederick A. Stokes Co., New York, 1938, page 80

296 Frank Bryan and John McClaughry, *The Vermont Papers*, Chelsea Green Publishing Co., 1990, pages 242–243

297 David A. Donath, "The Vermont Destination: Working Landscape and Bucolic Retreat," *The Vermont Difference, Perspectives from the Green Mountain State*, The Woodstock Foundation and The Vermont Historical Society, 2014

298 "Seeking to Ensure the Future Viability of Vermont's Dairy Industry," Report of the 33rd Grafton Conference, March 6–7, 2008 & December 6-7, 2008, The Windham Foundation, Grafton, Vermont

299 "Chasing Seeds: The Story of Vermont's Forgotten Abenaki Food System," Abenaki Arts & Education Center, abenaki-edu.org

300 "1850 AgCensus," USDA Census of Agriculture Historical Archive, agcensus.library.cornell.edu

301 "List of Vermont Apple Growers of Over 5 Acres in 1930," *Fifteenth Biennial Report of the Commissioner of Agriculture of the State of Vermont, 1928–1930*, E. H. Jones, Commissioner, pages 128-133

302 "List of Creameries and Cheese Factories, State of Vermont," *Twenty-Fourth Vermont Agricultural Report by The State Board of Agriculture for The Year 1904*, C. J. Bell, Secretary of the Board, Press of the Economist Co., Troy, N.Y., 1904, pages 149–155

303 Rev. G. F. Wright, "The Farmer's Future," a paper delivered at a meeting of the State Board of Agriculture at St. Albans, Vt., March 6th and 7th, 1872. In his paper, he stated "it is useless for the Vermont farmer to compete with those of the West in raising those few staples of the product that can be naturally raised in the West and that will bear storing and transportation without risk of injury and without too much expense." He went on to say "that the Vermont farmer has a substantial hold on the future. His soil, his climate, his abundance of pure water, and his proximity to markets of the growing cities and villages, give him unrivaled facilities for success. Only those who will prosper use their minds in studying how to cater to the demands of this growing market and this changing state of things."

304 The criteria were environmental and ecological quality; social and cultural integrity; condition of historic building and archaeological sites; aesthetic appeal; quality of tourism management; and outlook for the future. Vermont's anti-billboard law and the Vermont Housing and Conservation Board (VHCB) were cited as two key factors in the ranking.

305 "There has been a continuous decrease in the number of farms operating and the number of cows in New England for the last thirty years due to unattractive returns," from the *Biennial Report of the Vermont Commissioner of Agriculture, 1920–1922*, page 54.

306 Edwin C. Rozwenc, *Agricultural Policies in Vermont, 1860–1945*, page 174

307 Ibid, page 176

308 Lyman W. Peet of Cornwall, Vt, "Eastern and Western Farming," a paper presented to the State Board of Agriculture in 1883-1884, said, "only by the use of greater skill and capital by which production shall be cheapened with a quality so superior as to command the highest price in the market, can we hope successfully to meet Western competition."

309 Melissa Pasanen, "Best Cheeses: Vermont," Culture: the word on cheese, January 15, 2019, culturecheesemag.com

310 "Brewery Trails," Vermont Brewers Association, vermont brewers.com

311 "Vermont Cheese Trail," Vermont Cheese Council, vtcheese.com

312 See "Strolling of the Heifers 2019 Locavore Index ranking the 50 states in terms of their commitment to healthy local food." It was an index published annually beginning

in 2012 by the former Strolling of the Heifers in Brattleboro, Vermont. See "How Committed Is Your State to Local Food?", Cornucopia Institute, cornucopia.org

313 "History of the Working Lands Enterprise Initiative—Vermont," workinglands .vermont.gov

314 Ellie French, "Report: Vermont spent $285 million over 10 years supporting the dairy industry," *VTDigger*, May 10, 2021

315 "Governor Scott proposes significant investments in agriculture," *Vermont Business Magazine,* Jan. 23, 2023, vermontbiz.com

316 Tyler Resch, "Future of Farming in Vermont May Include Small Scale Farms," *Brattleboro Reformer*, Feb. 25, 1977, page 5

317 "Agriculture Focus Group, Report To Governor's Commission On The Economic Future Of Vermont, November 1989," stated, "Agriculture in Vermont is threatened. If it is to be strengthened for its significant economic impact, for its contribution to tourism and industry through maintenance of the landscape, or because it perpetuates respected cultural traditions, a positive financial plan must be developed that gives farmers a greater chance for success."

318 "A 2018 Exploration of the Future of Vermont Agriculture, Ideas to Seed a Conversation and a Call to Action," produced by University of Vermont Extension and the Vermont Housing & Conservation Board, Oct. 2018

319 Ben Laine, CoBank Knowledge Exchange, Oct. 31, 2018

320 K. Charles Ling, "Dairy Cooperative Growth Challenges: Technology, Ingredients and Equity Financing," *USDA Rural Development, Research Report 2016*, May 2005

321 A study funded by the Vermont Department of Education in 2010 (see Growing Jobs Vermont Style) recommended a number of options, going forward, to address agricultural educational needs in Vermont. Some of the suggestions include having public and private institutions, including the Community College, partnering around a food-based mission: clustering educational hubs around the Career Centers; having a curriculum on sustainable agriculture for high schools such as the Center for Integrated Agricultural Systems has done at the University of Wisconsin; providing internships; increasing the collaborative model like that established with the 2 plus 2 programs; having a middle college such as in Europe for an associate degree; and expanding life-long learning opportunities and establishing certificate programs.

322 Thomas L. Daniels, Kyle McCarthy, & Mark B. Lapping, "The Fragmenting Countryside and the Challenge of Retaining Agricultural Land: The Vermont Case," *Society of Natural Resources* 36 (1), https://doi.org/10.1080/08941920.2022.2132438

323 Jake Claro, "Local Food Economic Impacts in Vermont," Cornell Small Farms Program, January 8, 2018, at smallfarms.cornell.edu/2018/01/local-food -economic-impacts/

324 Nancy Everhart and Alissa White, "Vermont Agriculture & Food System Plan 2021–2030: Payment for Ecosystem Services," agriculture.vermont.gov/document/ vermont-agriculture-and-food-system-strategic-plan-2021-2030